How Is This My Life?

Confessions of a Sane Single Woman

Cover design: J. René Creative
Silhouette: © Untashable / Shutterstock
Editors: Kimberly Reszetylo
           J. Rene Creative

To my beautiful and devoted mother, thank you for your continued love and support. There will never be a closer, more fundamental relationship than ours. I love you with my entire heart.

To my paternal unit, ummm, thanks for knocking up my mother? Yeah... that's about it.

CHAPTER 1
who let the dogs out?

It's happening again. Sex. Loud, obnoxious, *why is it waking me up at 2 a.m. again* SEX! The sound of her headboard violently banging on our shared wall is accompanied by a bed frame squeaking like an antique passed down from great grandmother herself. Constant screeching. Hell, maybe that's *her* and not even the bed frame. The water in the glass I keep on my nightstand is trembling in ripples every time my wall shakes from the impact like a whole damn T-Rex is about to stomp into my room at any second now.

"SHUT UP!" I scream, banging on the wall behind me like they care that I have to be at work in only four hours. In my bedroom, softly illuminated by the glow of the outside street lights, I'm now wide awake listening to my neighbor's nightly love sessions with her on-again/off-again baby daddy. Yes, even though they just finished fighting because he was "texting some bitch in his car." She has very little going for herself – a mildly attractive blonde white girl with a booty, but she has a man despite her nondescript looks and overall lack of ambition.

On the other hand, I have everything going for myself, yet somehow the only reliably affectionate male in my life is a cat. Something is so wrong here. *I* should be the one crying out in orgasmic bliss to the point of vocal instability, not lying here listening to *her* love cries - alone. Though it *does* sound good. And he *is* pretty hot. Maybe I could... *nope, I never replaced those batteries. Shit!*

Well, I'm not falling back asleep anytime soon. Who can I call? Ariah. She will be so mad if her phone rings right now, but then again, "mad" is her default setting regardless, and I need to vent to someone, dammit. I fumble through the gold 1200 thread count Egyptian cotton sheets to find my home phone. Yes, I am among the maybe eighteen people in America who still uses a landline, which I prefer to distribute to potential suitors instead of my cell number. Oddly enough though, I once had a man stop talking to me, stating that he couldn't take me seriously because he only had my landline and not my cell phone number. That made almost no sense to me because, in reality, it should have made him take me *more* seriously. I explained to him that when my home phone rings, his name comes up across not only all of the televisions that are in use, but also three different phones would ring with his name on the caller ID, and of course, the main phone loudly verbally announces who is calling. So, if I were married or had a trail of men all up and through my place, they would *all* know that he is calling me *right now*. Apparently, he lacked the common sense to grasp any of that and never spoke to me again. But that's fine because I prefer a man who is smarter than my phone anyway.

I locate the cordless device near the foot of my bed to call my girl, praying she doesn't call me a...

"BITCH! Do you know what time it is?"

I saw that coming.

"Girl, I need to buy a house," I say desperately.

"I KNOW you did not call me at two in the damn morning to discuss your real estate needs. I'm hangin' up!"

"Wait! No! The neighbors are having sex again and it woke me," I grumble. "I'm out of batteries."

"Ooooh girl, it sounds that good that you need the *toys*? Put the phone up to the wall! Lemme hear!"

"Eww! Now *I'm* hangin' up!"

"Look, you called *me*! Next time call Diego" Click. Silence. Damn.

Did that harlot just hang up on me? But I can't even blame her. After all, I did just call her at official booty call hours, so she probably thought she was about to get some yum yum. I'm definitely going to hear about this in the morning. As sweet and reserved as Ariah is, she has her fiery moments, and interrupting her sleep is a guaranteed way to spark all of them. I know better.

Ariah and I met in graduate school where we were among five of the only Black females in the program. I'm the loud, volatile, and outgoing to her quiet, subtle, and introverted nature, but damn it, we were going to become friends whether she liked it or not. I could be wrong, but I believe it was around our third lunch together when she realized she needed my particular brand of dysfunction in her life. She likely could've done without choking on her sandwich while listening to me relive a nightmare, I mean date, I had gone on the weekend before, but someone needed to hear about poor Michael.

I was waiting for Mike at the ice cream shop, anticipating the giant Oreo cone I was about to abandon my diet to devour. An indulgence this sweet had been a long time coming! Punctuality is my middle name, so I was ten minutes early, but he was already ten minutes late. I loathe tardiness and it definitely tops my list of turn-offs. Also, the person on the receiving end of the delay shouldn't have to reach out to learn *why* s/he is being kept waiting. Total lack of consideration. So I made the call only to find out that he was halfway here when it suddenly dawned on him that it would probably be unwise to bring his three barking dogs, so he turned around to take them home. *Pardon me, sir, but we never discussed canines. I had no idea that you had one, let alone THREE. You don't even know if I like dogs, but you were going to bring the entire pack along on our first date. Wonderful!*

Mike finally arrived forty-five minutes late, which of course, annoyed me to no end because it was a humid, blistering 87-degree day in southwestern Pennsylvania. I was dressed for it in a short white skirt and equally pristine white Adidas kicks. Though pink generally goes against my fashion religion, I decided to try something new. Eighteen inches of luxurious natural hair was pulled up into a glorious crown of semi-tight curls sitting easily five inches atop my head with a pink flower to accent my seasonal look. As he finally pulled up, I felt confident in my appearance for this first meeting.

Don't turn the car radio down or anything. Just blast your music with explicit lyrics and anger all the parents with young children at the shop. Heads turned, whispers and stares, the works.

He stepped out of his car several inches shorter than the height he'd boasted, but it was fine because he wasn't an ugly guy. His shirt was a little too small though. At first glance, he appeared well-built, but upon closer inspection, I realized it was nothing but fuscle, as Ariah calls it. You know, when it looks like it *could* be muscle but it's really just a lot of fluff covering all the muscles? I don't mind a little thickness, though.

So we exchanged our nice-to-meet-you hug and chatted while waiting in line to order our ice cream. The only benches available were unshaded, so we took a seat fully prepared to brave the scorching heat. We would need to eat quickly to avoid a melted mess. While I sat wishing for some more wind, I noticed that Mike had hazel eyes that sparkled in the sun, but he also had a very bald head that was beginning to perspire. No. Let's just be honest. He was dripping with sweat, melting faster than his chocolate ice cream cone. He ran to the car to find the towel that every bald man keeps handy for this exact reason. As he began to wipe his head, I noticed something odd. This bald man had mysteriously acquired a full head of *hair*!

Because his head wasn't freshly shaven, his entire dome was completely *covered* in dog hair that attached itself to the stubble, which made it look like he was wearing a bad toupée! When I brought the situation to his attention, he then began to frantically wipe off his head and shake out the hair-covered towel. Well of course as he does that, because karma hates me *so* much, the wind that I had been wishing for all afternoon began to briskly blow and who is downwind? You got it. This girl. I was screaming frantically for him to stop as three dogs-worth of hair flew into my mouth, all over my ice cream, and throughout my carefully styled curly hair! He finally realized what was happening and hurried to try to shake out my hair, which almost caused him to lose a limb. *NEVER touch a Black woman's natural curls*. By doing that, it only worked in the dog hair deeper and tangled it up even more in my hair.

He offered to buy me more ice cream. *No thanks*. He offered to make it up to me with another outing. *No thanks*. I went home and had Wash Day all. over. again. For those of you who don't understand the exasperation in that sentence, it means I went home to spend *another* seven hours washing, conditioning, detangling, re-twisting, and drying a foot and a half of natural, tight, curly hair. Oh, and let's not forget the dog hair removal.

In silence, Ariah stared at me with her lower jaw dangling in shock, then finally said, "That can't seriously be true!"

"Could I make that up?"

"Yes, bitch!! YES," she said, laughing with a mouth full of food.

Like so many of my friends, she's always calling me a bitch and she's not wrong – I *am* an inventive soul but I *wish* I were making up these dates! When I showed her the photo of the dog hair all twisted up in my hair before I washed it, she couldn't deny my story was, in fact, true. We've been super cool ever since; but after that middle of the night non booty-call I just made, we might not be *that* cool.

But even if Ariah *is* pissed, it doesn't make her any less right; I called the wrong person. Complaining to her about being all hot and bothered is pointless when Diego is absolutely more qualified to fix the problem. 6'3", light caramel complexion, body like something straight from a Greek mythology tale, and can eat my, ahem, snack box like a starving man who robbed a deli! Inked down his entire left side, Diego can deliver that Puerto Rican thug-style ecstasy that makes my entire body weak and my brain lose all sense of purpose! In his mouth lay talent that should be bottled and sold in fine department stores and nothing would inspire world peace more than him filling arenas worldwide and teaching the entire male population how to artfully, effectively, and proficiently eat that snack box! But I would never actually call him for that – I'm far too modest, believe *that* or not. When it happens, it's usually only because he randomly stops by for a visit. We've known each other forever and don't really date or have actual sex but damn, I would drain my entire 401k right now for a knock on that door from him.

Every part of me wants to lay here and see if I can vocally out-sex my neighbors myself, sans batteries, but that would just be childish. And seriously, how are her kids not awake? These walls are paper thin. *I should leave some tools on her porch for her lying, cheating boyfriend to at least tighten that bed frame so I don't have to hear all the squeaking.*

Tomorrow's TO-DO list: Buy liquor, earplugs, and batteries

CHAPTER 2
a typical workday

It wouldn't be a normal day if my mother weren't randomly texting, video chatting, or calling me at some ungodly hour in the morning. I'm trying to get myself together, however, I'm still exhausted from all the sexual activity I *didn't* have last night. But of course, Mother is wide awake and ringing my phone.

"Good morning Mother," I croak, sounding like a 46-year-old man. I *just* woke up; I don't have my sexy lady tones warmed up yet.

"Oooh, why do you sound like that? What are you doing?"

"It's 4:30 am. I'm getting ready for work... and ovulating it feels like. What are *you* doin'?"

"Uhhh, finding a man to send to your *house* - git me some grandbabies."

"Nope. It's *way* too early for this. Love you. Goodbye."

Though we have an extremely close relationship, the frequency with which I have had to abruptly end conversations with my mother has increased lately because, in her old age, she now has *no* filter and couldn't care less about tact.

I drag myself into work completely devoid of functionality. I feel like I might have put on make-up but I think I missed a spot – like my entire face! I may or may not have both my contacts in and where is my lunch? Still on the counter at home. This is going to be a tragically long day, but it's business as usual under the harsh fluorescent lights of the fifth floor's large open space.

As I ignore three calls, two voicemails, and a text message from Ariah, undoubtedly telling me how foul I am for my late-night call, a colleague pops her head into my cubicle. There aren't many work visits that I welcome, but my teammate Summer is always a treat.

"Wow, you're lookin' wrecked up today. Thank God it's Friday!"

Ok, maybe not ALWAYS a treat.

"Thank you, *Winter*."

"Touché!"

"Well, warm up your icy-ass disposition when you come through my cube and maybe I'll call you by your name. What do you need, Miss *Summer*?"

Despite that questionable entrance, Summer's personality is as inviting and refreshing as her name suggests. Her blonde hair, bright blue eyes, and warm smile sound like something totally fabricated, but her kind heart and sweet, bubbly temperament are as real as her adorable features.

"So, I'm having a bad day," Summer whines.

"How? The day just started? And look at *you*. Now look at *me*. Who is having the bad day here? Like, I think I lost my right eye's false lash in the parking lot!"

Summer stares intently at me, so I frown and stare skeptically back at her.

"Looks like you lost them *both*! Haha! So hey, like I said, I'm having a bad day - well, week really. I need you to cheer me up, so tell me something funny; you always make me laugh. Go ahead." She then takes a seat and plops her chin into the palm of her hand like a bored five-year-old waiting to exit time out.

"Summ, I had to listen to my neighbors get nasty all night. Sex that I haven't had in like two years. And if you count *good* sex, even longer than *that*! I've got nothing funny to say right now. I'm tired."

"So yeah, that's pretty sad. We need to get you laid! Oooh! How about one of your dates! You always have such horribly bad dates that are always *so* funny. Tell me about one of those," She says, visibly bouncing in her chair.

Stupefied. With raised eyebrows, I look to my left, then to my right – is this girl talking to *me*? I am studying her face while confusion is written all over mine, as my face doesn't hide emotion well. I'm waiting for Ashton Kutcher to jump out and tell me I'm being Punk'd, because I am positive she did not just ask me to tell her about my horrific love life to lift her spirits and brighten her damn day.

I stare blankly at Summer while she grins at me like a child waiting for a cookie. Fine. I will regale this young woman with one of my recent dates so she will take her ass out of my cube and back to her own work. But which one? There have been so many lately. It would never be thought possible for one woman to meet so many dysfunctional men, but I am here. It is me. I am the "one woman." Men are so quick to tell us that if a woman reaches a certain age and still isn't married that it must be *her*, not the men. I am here to heavily debate that theory.

We all have our own unique set of dating experiences, some good, some... well... not so much. It's how we deal with the negative experiences in order to move on to the next, hopefully, more positive one. However, what if there were never that next, more positive one? What if one after the other, these men all behaved as though they were *hatched* somewhere, raised by a cackle of hyenas, and were never able to learn basic consideration and how to treat a lady? These are the men who find me and ask staggering questions like, "Why would I open your doors for you?" Umm, how about chivalry and courtesy to name a few, both of which have apparently died and been buried under my porch.

I never expected to be in this situation - over 35, multiple degrees, but single and childless. I had fully anticipated being married with two children by the age of 27. I'm a few years behind schedule. Really, at this point, I'm like a rare commodity. My best guy friend, Tyce, often tells me that I'm intimidating to men - that when a man sees a beautiful woman, well-put-together, and handling her business, if he's not on her level, he may feel emasculated. Valid point, but how is it my problem that I got my shit together and they chose not to do so? No excuses please; Tyce and I were both raised by single parents in the projects and went on to obtain master's degrees and careers.

I'm not necessarily even looking for someone on my formal educational level. I would just be content if I could communicate with him on some sort of functional level. Unlike the conversation I had a few weeks ago with a man I met online. When asked what he enjoys for fun, he told me that he enjoyed festabowls and stuff. Please sir, what the hell is a festabowl? Is it Mexican? Is there chicken or rice involved? He replied, "You know, with the rides and foods and activities – festabowls!" Ohhh, FESTIVALS. Ok. Then this text exchange occurred which forced me to determine just *how* open to giving chances I really was.

Him: My toof hurts. Should I go to the ER?

Me: No you should go to the dentist.

Him: Naw cuz I got a cavity n they jus gon try n take my toof out!

Me: No, if it's a cavity, they will just fill it.

Him: Oh, ok.

"OH, OK?" Seriously? Because this is just common knowledge to people who go to the dentist regularly, so now I'm forced to wonder what the hell's happening in that mouth of his!

Him: You know any open on weekends?

Me: Only one that I can think of but I wouldn't recommend them

Him: Ok, where is dey at?

Long, hard pause so I can determine if that whole sentence really just happened.

Him: Hello? U still there?

Give him the benefit of the doubt. Maybe he just can't spell. But he sounded like just as much of an idiot in person as he did in written form so he definitely won't be receiving an invitation to the company Christmas party.

I would even settle for someone with just a bit of damn sense, unlike the gentleman who expressed genuine concern that my cat was lonely and bored while I was at work. I told him that the kitty was cool, but he insisted that couldn't possibly be the case and said that when he came to meet me, he was going to bring and release a bag of LIVE crickets in my apartment to relieve my pet's boredom. CRICKETS!? Are you *crazy*!? Do you have any idea how much noise *one* cricket makes, let alone a *family* of those bouncy little bastards!? And let me stop you right there because I know what you're thinking. No, he was *not* joking; he was dead-ass serious. He lived around the corner from the pet store and everything. Needless to say, he was never invited over.

So, no Ashton Kutcher. No hidden cameras. Summer is still sitting here awaiting my tale of woe that will inevitably bring her delight. Fine.

I begin to tell her about Kevin, who I had been having phone conversations with for a few weeks. We met online and he had an appealing profile with nice photos, so I was planning to meet him downtown for ice cream. It really is the perfect date – if the person you're meeting is crazy and busted up in the face, you get a baby cone, eat it fast, and the date ends quickly. If the person resembles their photos & doesn't smell strange, you can get a normal size cone, eat it at a functional pace, and maybe take a walk and draw it out.

So the night before our meeting, I asked Kevin, "What's wrong with you?" Yes, I just came out and asked because the reality of the situation is, when I see a man, I'm going to immediately *know* what's wrong with him so he should just save me some time and tell me now. As I said previously, I wear my entire thought process on my face. One will always know what I'm thinking without a word spoken, so I would really just prefer to not have to try to mute my face. He told me nothing was wrong with him. I gave him one more opportunity to come clean and I inquired again, "You looked in the mirror this morning and didn't see *anything* that was amiss? Everything was in the right place?" He assured me that he was good to go and turned the question around to me.

Everything here is intact. Though I have always had some insecurity surrounding my skinny calves and my derrière that isn't nearly as thick as the stereotypical "Black-girl booty," I make up for it with thick thighs and full, supple breasts that would make the Godly mountain ranges green with envy. I wouldn't describe myself as cute - my features are far too piercing; but at the very least visually intriguing. Many have called me beautiful but I have never felt that way. However, my long, natural hair, full lips, and almond-shaped eyes that penetrate the deepest recesses of one's soul will absolutely turn a few heads.

So basically, I told him I was cool.

It was go time! I was walking down the street and I thought I saw him – tall, dark chocolate lookin' like a mouthwatering appetizer. His clothes were ironed and he was ever so crisp. Khakis creased, a sky blue button-down shirt tucked in which displayed his tremendous physique, with a camel-colored belt that matched the casual shoes; he was on point. As he drew nearer, I noticed that both his hair and facial hair were clean-cut with a full goatee and chinstrap. When he recognized me, he smiled and those teeth were just as straight and white like he was raised by dentists. When he pressed his taut body against mine, that hug was perfection and he smelled intoxicating. OMG, can this man be real? I have never met anyone online who showed up looking as functional as his profile suggested.

I took off my sunglasses so he could see my striking green eyes and when he removed his, one eye looked dead at ME and the other eye was looking at the lady across the street! My whole face fell all the way apart. I could feel the shock visibly forming across it and worked diligently to control it but it was simply beyond me at that point. *Close your mouth, girl!* As I stared at this situation that seemed to be happening now in slow motion, I was formulating a plan to determine which eye I was supposed to be looking into. Then it hit me! Look at the eye that's looking at me! *Good Plan!* But shit, that other one is just wandering around – is it coming back? *Control your damn FACE and look at the good eye!* This is so much work. And I stood there wondering how he looked in the mirror and claimed to notice nothing was "off."

"Bahahahahaha!!" Summer is laughing uncontrollably in my cubicle at this point which is now drawing attention from other colleagues. I think it is safe to say that she is now having a better day. "I am dead, Renée. You are *so* funny! You need to write a book!"

I hear that a lot.

"So, what happened? Did you ever see him again or did you cut it off 'cause you couldn't get past his 'wandering eye?' Hahahahaha!"

Actually, I *did* see him again because he was a guy with a great sense of humor. But it all came to a head one day at lunch when I inquired about his previous relationship.

He explained that he thought she was cheating on him, so he felt the need to investigate. He told me all about this nagging feeling in the pit of his stomach one night that caused him to jump up and run out of the house in what he was wearing. Since he made specific mention of it, I just *had* to know about this man's attire. Kevin told me that he had on boxers, a robe, and his work boots and hopped on his bike to ride over to his girl's house. I had to stop him to clarify because this was almost too much for me.

"You had on *only* boxers, a robe, and boots?"

"Yes."

"And you rode your motorcycle over to her house to confront her and this guy you thought she was sleeping with in the middle of the night?"

"Motorcycle!? I don't have a motorcycle! I rode my bicycle over there."

Wait, WHAT!? So yeah, that was the end of me and Kevin. You can't tell a woman that you rode a bicycle across town in a robe and boxers and expect her to still think you're even remotely sane. That is the epitome of instability!

Summer is now in my cube in tears with laughter and can barely catch her breath. Since she has such a pale complexion, she has turned an apple shade of red and is reaching for my tissues to dry her tears to prevent her thick mascara from running. I snatch them away quickly before she can reach them. Too much joy is being had from my miserable dating life, so her make-up deserves to run a tad. Then she can look as rough as I do today.

She exits still giggling, delighted that her day was made brighter at my expense as I sit thinking, *Damn. This sucks.* Summer is not the first to request to hear my tragic dating stories for a "feel better" laugh, and I'm positive she won't be the last. They are so unbelievable that you would think I'm making them up, but sadly, they are all true. When do I get to tell someone about an actual romance story? One that doesn't come with strings attached or because he messed up so badly that a grand gesture is necessary to repair the damage.

After some time passes with me half-working and half-fantasizing about getting a Costco-sized supply of those batteries later, I hear Summer's perky voice behind me yet again.

"Renée, I need you to tell that story just *one* more time!"

"Summer, I am *not* telling you that…" and as I turn around mid-sentence to face her, there is not one but *four* additional girls standing there with looks of excitement and anticipation on all of their faces, like they are about to hear the greatest story ever told – I am *not* the Bible. *I hate you, Summer.*

Add to my TO-DO list: Find a work-from-home job

CHAPTER 3
std's & bad decisions

A new week has come and I never did get those batteries. After work today, definitely. Fortunately, the neighbor and her boy toy were on hiatus over the weekend so I was able to catch up on my sleep, but I was afraid to fall too deep because my whole living situation is a nightmare!

While reading on my porch this past Saturday afternoon, enjoying the warm sun beating down on my bare feet, my peace and solitude had been momentarily interrupted by a slender, angry-looking woman stomping down the sidewalk. My head dipped ever so slightly as I nonchalantly hid my face behind the novel, every so often peeking around the pages as she headed in my general direction. *Damn it, why don't I have my shades!* Being the drama-free, yet curious neighbor I am, I was intrigued and dying to know where she was headed, because girlie was on a warpath! She was about to do some damage somewhere and as long as it wasn't *here*, it was all good. The closer she came to me, the more pissed off she appeared – and she was way overdue for a new hair weave. Eyes wide, I peered over the top of my riveting new Edmund Okocha murder mystery as her hostility hung a right and headed down my block! *Oh damn! She's going to my neighbor's house! I gotta see this!* Before I could even get out of my seat to slide my shoes on to 'take a leisurely walk' but really just be nosey, I heard her bellow at maximum volume, "Your *man* gave me gonorrhea!"

Well damn, that wasn't on my crazy bitch bingo card. Fuming explained. She shouted that out giving *zero* cares that a mass of people just overheard those wild proclamations about her current sexual health status. This angry woman rolled up to my neighbor's apartment to confront her with this information in front of both of her young children, who were still playing in their green turtle sandbox beside the porch.

My trashy neighbor sucked her teeth. "No, he didn't!"

Oh for real? Because you were there, huh? I wonder if this was the same "bitch he was texting in the car" from a while back. If so, she probably would've preferred to receive flowers from him instead of the gift she's claiming he gave her.

"He absolutely *did* and you ain't nothin' but a nasty whore who probably got gonorrhea too!"

This verbal berating of my neighbor's sexual character went on for a while and I couldn't help but find myself thinking, *if you knew he was someone else's man, why were you having sex with him? And where were the condoms if you know about her alleged nastiness?* I had a whole unopened box upstairs I could've given her. Lord knows I'm not getting any! Would've had to blow the dust off of them and check the expiration date, but it's definitely too late now.

Neighbors began to gather outside to watch as these women verbally assaulted each other over a man-child who isn't worth the dirt that they were standing on. Foul language was being hurled all over the complex as her two boys observed in fear for their mother's safety. The confrontation got physical when the contagious woman jacked my neighbor up against the wall, still roaring obscenities. She was then chased into her apartment with her two kids. The hostile lady with gonorrhea finally decided to leave and still needed to have some last words even though the person they were directed toward could no longer hear them. I couldn't help but selfishly think, *Great, this should buy me some extra sleeping time. If he's out here spreadin' itchies, drippies, and scratchies, there will be no sex! And if there IS? Well, she's just as nasty as that girl said!*

♀ ♂ ♀ ♂

Hot damn! I've waited all day to get to the battery section! Sell me stock, please. How does a lady own this many pleasure devices and not one of them is in working order? I'm thinking that to power everything, I'll need at least three sizes of batteries. I should just invest in one that plugs in. I knew it was bad when we were in the weekly meeting and the Team Sports department pulled out their new sample collection of signature baseball bats and it made my mind go to its naughty place. Though I must admit the tingles below subsided temporarily when I watched my colleague dig deep enough into her ear to scratch the temporal lobe of her brain, pull the finger out to *stare* at it for way too long, then discreetly *smell* the finger! The most disturbing part about this is that she, too, has a man! Someone put a *ring* on that funky finger! I simply don't pull weirdness out of my body and sniff it. And if that *were* on the agenda, it damn sure wouldn't be in public. Yet somehow I'm still painfully single – I will never understand it.

As I mosey through the produce section, I am approached by a man who is talking to me like he ain't neva seent a English class in his LYFE. Yes, those words are how I *feel* in my soul hearing it. I'm working diligently to translate the words that *seem* to be English, but it's work! He then proceeds to criticize my fresh fruit purchase by informing me, "You 'on't need all'at. You too damn skinny already, Muffin." WTF!? Did you just call me muffin? REALLY!?? *I'm too damn tired for all this BS! But since he mentioned it, muffins DO sound good though.*

Of course I'm standing in a fairly long line to checkout because WHY after work hours would a large chain retailer want to open more than two lanes at once? I always feel like I'm forgetting something, but I have everything, I think - batteries, earplugs, bananas... For my smoothie – don't be nasty. I know it's been a while but damn. Give me some credit. *Ugh, seven people in front of me - by the time I check out, these bananas will be ripe.* Then out of nowhere while deep in my own random thoughts about rush hour traffic and tacos, I hear a raspy, but deep voice say, "Heyyy pretty hair gurrl!"

Please let this very large guy in the nylon wind suit with the gold grill and half-dreads, half-bald head NOT be talking to me. It never fails; I get hit on, catcalled, whatever'd by *the* most unsuitable candidates in the building! The model of man perfection will walk right past me, but the dude with more nose hair than eyebrows? Oh, he's in love with me at first sight. *Just ignore it, Renée. If you ignore it, it will go away. Like bullies and ghosts.*

Besides, he's probably not even talking to you, right? Right. Wrong.

"HEYYY PRETTY HAIR GURRL!"

Oh my gosh, it's getting louder! By now, the white people are starting to look to me for an answer to this hot mess because I am the only other person of color in the line and ironically, I do happen to have the prettiest hair in it. At work earlier, Summer *did* let me know that it looked like I had both of my eyelashes today, so I must've been doing something right appearance-wise, but now I'm wishing I had done it all wrong again. So I finally look up to acknowledge this person screaming through the line at me.

"Yo name Ty'Reisha right?"

"No"

"You sure?"

I'm *sure* all this yelling across the store is stereotypical and inappropriate. I'm *sure* I'm embarrassed right now and that *nobody* wants to hear this hot mess. I'm *sure* I need you to pick a hairstyle and commit, please. And I'm *sure* I know my name, sir.

"Yup, I'm positive."

"Oh cuz you had lookted like this girl I had messed wit' name Ty'Reisha. Ok well could I take you out sometiiime though?"

Oh, would you look at that! Lane four just opened up! Let me, my pretty hair, and my earplugs that I should've used to avoid *that* conversation get the hell out of here! As I pass by him again, he's finally checking out, paying for hot dogs in change, which makes me wonder how he was planning to pay for our date had I said yes.

I often wonder about the fiscal responsibility of some of the men I've met. They all seem to want to be the leader of the relationship but couldn't lead a bird to the sky. I've worked too hard for my stellar credit to have some aimless creature leading me into financial ruin. For instance, I have met at least three men who didn't have transportation, specifically because they either couldn't afford, didn't want, or didn't "believe in" car payments, but the decisions they made surrounding their lack of cars were red flags. I have also learned that those men I've encountered who didn't "believe in" car payments usually didn't because they couldn't afford them. My friend Julia doesn't believe in car payments either but she and her husband make a solid, sturdy six-figure salary that allows her to be able to charge her new vehicle to her Visa, then pay it off at the end of the month like a boss bitch. These men don't have the boss part, just the bitch!

One guy didn't have a car, he just Ubered everywhere because his license was suspended. He said it should be back sometime this year, as soon as he finishes paying the thousands of dollars in fines. So I was curious as to how long it had been suspended and he explained, just over twenty years! That seems excessive to me, but maybe that's standard? No. He got a DUI and his license was suspended, but he drove anyway. He got pulled over again and got another DUI which lengthened the suspension. He did this a few times until he realized he should probably just stop drinking and driving altogether. And instead of putting the money toward the fines, he's paying for the Uber. At this point, I question his overall judgment, so he does not get to lead our hypothetical relationship.

The second gentleman was saving for a car and told me he had just over $8,000 set aside. I was thinking ok, he must be almost there with his savings to get himself a car. When asked what he was saving to purchase, he said a new Ford F-150. Sir, that truck is 39k, you have 8k. You will be in an Uber for the rest of your life. Come to find out, between work, shopping, and miscellaneous trips, he was spending just over $350/mo. on an Uber plus putting money aside for this truck. I know my math is not that bad. If you combine those two amounts, you pretty much have a car payment to have your own vehicle to come & go as you please.

And the third, well, he had been in jail for the past eighteen years. Oh my bad, not consecutively; he went for three, got out, then went *back* for thirteen, got out, then went back *again* for another two years. He can't lead our hypothetical relationship because he can't stay out of jail long enough!

Don't even get me started on the ones who are trying to date me but don't own a car *or* have access to one, talkin' about some, "Come scoop me up." Sir, I drive a Hyundai, not a Taxi. I understand that they both end in "i" but they are not synonymous. Picture it. Pittsburgh. City of hills, bridges, and tunnels, where it's winter like five months of the year. By the time I clean off my car, finally make it to you, and bring you *back* to my place because you live at home, whatever *you* planned to do to me sexually, I could have done to *myself, twice,* and been asleep. So no, I will NOT "come scoop you up."

These are just a few of the scenarios I think about that make me question how much more detailed I can be in my prayers tonight for God to send me someone half normal. He definitely needs to step in though, because the men my friends and family have sent me need a lot more than prayer!

My sister Neka set me up twice - once with a 36-year-old near-virgin who was 5'2" and sounded more feminine than *I* do on the phone. Then, there was the guy she claimed was SO fine! Like, SOO fine. Ok, well what's the problem (other than the fact that he was nowhere near fine)? He just got out of jail. As in yesterday, *just* got out. Twenty years. My bestie, Liza, put me on with a 43-year-old, bi-racial man who told me that he had never dated outside of his race before. Hold up. He's half black, I'm whole black. I am *not* outside of this man's race and the fact that he thinks I *am* is a subject for a whole other book. My girl Nadia hooked me up with a life coach, except he always wanted to life coach *me*. That shit was exhausting always having to maintain some super positive outlook. Damn it, I just want to eat cookie dough in sweats under my electric blanket and be left the hell alone some days!

My bed is awaiting my arrival so I can escape these crazy thoughts. As I close my eyes and teeter on the precipice of sleep, it's happening. The sex. Again! HOW!? *Didn't he JUST get done giving the neighbor an STD? Or are they called STIs now? Ugh, who CARES!? I'm just starting to feel like they're going to migrate into my apartment like little sexually transmitted roaches! I wonder if Amazon sells a full-body condom?*

"SHUT UUUPPP!!!" I scream in pointless frustration while banging uselessly on the wall behind me. *Ugh... How is this my LIFE?*

Add to tomorrow's TO-DO list: Go buy a damn house

CHAPTER 4
this is NOT like buying a car

I'm draggin' ass into Howard Hanna the next morning after another night from hell! First, the cacophonous fornication, then my neighbor's unruly toddlers were awake most of the night, tirelessly running barefoot through an apartment with no carpeting to help absorb sound. In an M. Night Shyamalan twist, next came a fight about more infidelity and a new pregnancy, followed by all of the even louder make-up sex. Just two weeks prior, I left a hand-written note in her mailbox that read:

Good Morning Apartment 11 -

I'm very pleased that you have a healthy and active sex life and your stamina is impressive. But I'm kindly asking that you please rearrange your bedroom so that the bed is not on our shared wall as I have kindly done. The violent loud banging of body parts against the wall jolts me awake two to three times per night! With that level of disruptive noise, the police WILL respond to noise complaints, at which point I will gladly play them the many audio recordings of the noise, moaning, and

banging that constantly awaken me on a nightly basis.
I don't want to call the police, I just want some peace
in my apartment and to sleep through the night.

Thank you,

Apartment 12

Though, me positioning my bed against a different wall is irrelevant because I can't find a man functional enough to *eat* with let alone have actual *sex* with. But clearly, my pleas for peace were dismissed. So I called off work this morning to go buy a house, because that's how this works, right? It's like buying a car? You see one you want and you put some money on it and then they finance you and done – you move in. Easy peasy. I got this!

"Ma'am, no. You don't *got* this. That's not how this works," explains a short, austere woman wearing glasses and a tight bun in her hair. *Damn it!* "First we need to run your credit and see how much a bank will loan you. Then a realtor will show you homes within that price range." *So I'm not buying a house today and moving by this weekend. I liked my way better.* This stern but efficient woman brings me a stack of papers that leads me to believe I will be here all damn day!

After filling out so many papers that I may have promised the company my first-born male, she returns to inform me that my credit is solid, despite my six-figure student loan debt. She also seems pleased to let me know that I was approved for $195,000 in financing which is more than enough for my area. I was pleased for a hot second but then as I thought about it, this right here is where I need the man in my life to be on my level in terms of fiscal responsibility. How was I financed for $195k when my annual salary is a super mere fraction of that? I sit in this office thinking about the fact that the mortgage is not the only bill, lady! The bank doesn't care about the car note, insurance, cable, phone, utilities? How about food? Do they care if I eat? No? And OMG what about my weekly massage!? This will never do. *She's crazy as hell if she thinks I'm about to be out here robbing people and working six jobs to pay the damn light bill.*

"What I need to happen is you cut that number in half, then take $20,000 off of *that* and find me a house in that price range, please. I will be awaiting your call. Thank you." She looked at me like I was insane as I walked out of that office knowing damn well they weren't about to have me all broke and tired trying to pay some crazy ass mortgage.

♀ ♂ ♀ ♂

It wasn't long before I received a call from the realtor's office with a few homes to visit. None were really up to par – especially the townhomes. I have no intention of ever living connected to anyone again! Luckily, my girl Alexis is a total whore for homes – she and her husband Lincoln buy a new one every few years because they can't seem to stop adding children and pets to the family. So I wasn't shocked when she showed up and introduced me to the wonderful world of open houses. She really is the best person to have on hand because she is so knowledgeable regarding what to look for and what is a hard pass. There was one house where I was telling her how much I enjoyed the design aesthetic; I liked how the basement wall slanted inward from the top, as she was steadily dragging me out of that house screaming, "NO!" reprimanding me like a bad dog. How was I supposed to know that meant the backyard was about to fall into the basement? Other than college in Cleveland, I have lived in the projects my entire life. There was no one to show me the ropes when it came to home ownership – well, except now I have Lexi.

Andrew, my realtor, is waiting as Lexi and I pull up to a red brick home on the corner across from a church. She knows me well enough to sense some level of disappointment.

"I can't live across from a church, Lex. I want to have and do *all* the sins and God is like *right* there watching and extra judging the sinning that I fully plan to execute all over that giant porch. Like, that's a great porch!"

Andrew's head turns toward the car when he hears that her laughter has officially overpowered the radio that is playing one of her eight children's Kid's Bop songs. In near hysterics, Lexi replies, "Who you gonna sin with? You can't find a *man*! Hahahaha! What? Are you gonna have some 'Self-Sin' on the porch? Let's go!"

Wow! Everyone in my life is a whole damn comedian!

"Excuse me, you must've forgotten about Diego. I have zero problem servin' him up some snack box on that porch. Lunch is served, bitch."

We giggle like school girls as Andrew unlocks the door and we enter the home's main space. It's so open and warm with plush carpeting and great natural light. I'm in love already.

"This is my house!" I exclaim with excitement!

"HEY! You can't *say* that. We just walked in." Lexi turns to the realtor, "She doesn't mean that, she's been drinking."

I look at Lexi, offended. *No, I haven't.*

She continues, "It could have termites. There could be radon. Water pressure could be trash. Dude, foundation issues. It's a thing! Remember?"

As my eyes excitedly dance around the cozy interior and envision all the décor potential, they stop at the main wall. "Yo. I'm totally making love in front of that fireplace."

Lexi slowly looks up at me from across the room. The realtor turns to look at me with a confused frown from the entryway. They look at each other, then both walk away leaving me alone in this large, open space to ponder my future color schemes and think naughty thoughts. *Well damn, I didn't say with YOU. Don't flatter yourselves!* But that's fine, they can abandon me because this is my house – I can *feel* it!

Fortunately, Andrew isn't a creepy realtor who is chomping at the bit to sell the house. Or maybe he is, but understands the value of letting his customers peruse the real estate freely and come to him with questions. Or maybe he is super aging and the 78 steps round trip from the basement to the attic were just a bit much. Either way, I am content strolling the four levels with Lex discussing the home and how it's large enough to add a few kids and pets and a man… Apparently, she still has jokes.

"Sooo, have you considered dating a white guy?"

Well, that came out of nowhere. Though married to her grey-eyed, high school sweetheart Lincoln, Alexis is a white girl who has always been much sought after by the chocolate boys in high school and even earlier. She has always had a significant amount of junk in her trunk which made me envious and them stupid. Combine that with a tiny waist and long, thick, dark tresses, and they were all confused when she chose to date skinny, shy Linc in high school. They would say, "That white boy ain't gonna know what to do with all that ass." Well, apparently he did. Twenty years later, they are still married with what feels like twelve kids at times but are really only four. Or five. Maybe Dennis is the dog? I can't keep track anymore.

"I *did* go out with a white boy. Bald head Tyler. Remember?"

Lexi claims I never told her about going out with Tyler, whom I also met online. He seemed cool enough, but he lived at home with his mother so that should've been a red flag. He sold me this story about job loss or whatever and I was feeling like giving people a chance, so I was willing to temporarily overlook it. We went mini golfing and had a decent time. The conversation flowed well and he had striking blue-grey eyes that were ridiculously dreamy.

I began to lose interest though when he told me that I could come stay with him at his mom's place because she gives him his privacy. Excuse me? Do you never plan on finding your own place? I do not plan to have relations with you while mother is watching Jeopardy in the next room and I am too damn old for a walk of shame out of your mama's house in the morning. But interest left the building and hopped a plane to New Mexico when he told me,

"Oh yeah, I've had sex with a man before, but it just wasn't for me."

Fortunately, it was over the phone so the muting of the face wasn't an issue. I could contort her any which way I wanted and not have to feign a diplomatic non-verbal response. I can appreciate a woman, but I don't need to have sex with her to know it's not for me. Lexi has a great ass and Ariah has sexy, long legs. But by no means do I have any desire to smack up, flip or rub anything down on any of my lady loves. Hugs, damn it. *We hug*. And I usually have to threaten Ariah to even do that!

People experiment sexually all the time, so that wasn't my primary concern. The larger issue for me was when he went on to explain how he believed that when two people love each other, they can have sex in a manner that's amenable to both parties. *Very true*. So basically he still wanted it from behind, but just not from a man. I mean I *completely* get it – I thoroughly enjoy my sex from behind as well – the ass smacking, the hair pulling, the sound his solid body makes thundering into mine. But in *my* relationships, I prefer to be on the receiving end of that storm system, so I have to draw the line somewhere. To help these guys find that line in the future, here are its exact coordinates: 80.26 latitude, and 40.59 longitude because none of that is going to work for me, personally.

It's so rare that Lexi is at a loss for words. She is just standing in the large finished basement facing me with her entire mouth pursed to the side. Silence. Then the heat kicks on.

"Well at least you know the boiler works?" she said in the form of a question because she is still so confused by the entire story. To top it off, after I decided I was done with him, he felt the need to send me an unsolicited dick pic that looked like raw chicken.

"I almost contracted salmonella from holding the phone! There was no way I would've been able to put that in my mouth."

We begin our trek back upstairs to find the realtor, as Lexi is laughing uncontrollably and repeating, "OMG Salmonella!" while wiping away her hysterical tears. "You need to write a book!"

"Okay this is my house, I want it," I announce with glee to the realtor.

He seems thrilled but is still just standing there. I'm expecting some action. Like, call someone. Do something so I can move in next week. Hop to, man! Because one more night in that apartment and my neighbor may end up as a missing person on the side of a milk carton!

Confused, I ask, "So... what now? Do you call somebody?"

"Well, we make an offer."

Maybe I'm crazy but I thought that's what I just did. I said I want the house. Please. That means call the owners, tell them I want it, call the bank. Right? Wrong, again.

He turns to Lexi, "How much did she drink?"

He then explains that I have to write him a check for $1,200 for the owners to show that I'm serious, fill out a thirteen-page document that offers up my second born child, pay for an inspection, pay for radon and termite testing, pay for an appraisal, then *pray* at the church across the street that it all comes back ok, otherwise, I lose all of my money and have to start over on a new house.

What the actual hell? That's a LOT that can go wrong and this is going to take forever. I'm never getting away from my horrible neighbor. Well at least for another 45-60 days.

Add to my TO-DO list: Figure out who is paying for all of this because I don't have it

CHAPTER 5
countdown to my escape

ONE MONTH LEFT

"**D**o you need to buy some mistletoe? Come here baby," Brie jokes as she holds a bulky sprig of the 'toe overhead and rubs on my nonexistent booty while trying to fake kiss me in the home section.

"Get the hell away from me with that thing. You know damn well if I kiss you back you gon' have an attitude!"

Really, Ruby Rose is more of my girl crush if I had to claim one. Brie is exotically sexy with grey eyes and a cute smile, but I would still prefer a man under my mistletoe. Though she is Black girl number three in the graduate program with myself and Ariah, she is the chocolate face I saw first! I sat in class waving at her like a whole fool so excited to see another person who looked like me. She waved back skeptically and sat behind me unaware of the friendship that would inevitably blossom. I always brought goodies & sweets to class and offered her some, so she nicknamed me "Snacks." *Rude.* The nickname then turned to "Rose" from the sitcom *The Golden Girls* when I suggested she apply for a vaguely worded DIRECTOR OF IT position that I found. I told her I don't know what the hell "it" is, but she definitely should call and find out because I think she'd be exceptional at whatever "it" is! Well, *this* harlot sat there smiling and let me finish praising how well I thought she could do "it" before informing me that the position was I.T., as in Information Technology. Ok, well how about including some punctuation? Damn! We still die laughing about that to this day.

My high school friend Jenna, who we had to drag out of her house to go early Christmas shopping with us, had to go all the way to Belize to find her husband to kiss under that mistletoe. She always tells me to travel more and I'll find him; but damn it, I shouldn't have to import a man. She might be on to something, though. She and her love, Marco, are so gooey it's simultaneously disgusting and adorable because it evokes all the feels of envy. "Mi amor," this... "Mi amor," that... I want amor! But I'm probably not going to find it in this women's section of JC Penney's.

We continue to roam the store to get some early gift ideas, even though I'm closing on a house in twenty-four days; I have no Christmas money. I'm the most indigent person in the mall right now.

Three of us are strolling, laughing, and talking. Then three abruptly becomes two. Jenna's fire-red hair whips around in search of me, but I have swiftly and silently disappeared! While searching, both Jenna and Brie eye up the tall glass of dark chocolate milk passing by them. Now they are feverishly hunting for me because there is a *man* afoot and it is everyone's mission to get me successfully paired.

Still in search, Brie finally notices an odd situation occurring in the fuller-figure women's section, so she grabs Jenna's attention. They gently approach whom they're assuming to be a woman wearing a tan, ¾-length puffer coat with a thick, fur-lined hood up and one black glove. The other is dangling at the wrist. This woman is holding up and intently examining a pink dress covered in the most hideous flowers known to nature.

"Is that her?" a confused Jenna asks Brie as they approach the woman.

"Bitch, is that you!?" Brie blurts out toward the coated figure.

"Shhh! Is he gone?" I whisper.

"Who?" they both lean in and whisper back.

"Big Black guy," I say in an urgent, hushed tone.

Brie and Jenna look at each other and shrug while I'm still holding up this tacky-ass dress like I'm planning to buy it for Nana.

"Oh, you mean that *fine* gentleman who just passed by? We need to go hunt him down! But why are we whispering, and why are you hiding like some kind of fugitive?" Jenna probed under her breath.

I immediately haul the girls to the furthest point in the mall food court and sit with my back to the masses so as not to be recognized by any passersby. While we scarf down New York-style pizza, I tell them about Nathan - ya know, sexual chocolate they just feasted their ogling eyes upon in the store over yonder?

Nate and I had spoken on the phone for about a week and a half before deciding to meet in person. Coincidentally, he worked in my hometown just eleven blocks away, even though he lived in the city. The plan was for me to pick him up after work and grab some what? Ice cream, of course. It was an unseasonably warm fall day, so after work, I came home, put myself back together, touched up my hair, and was out the door to meet the man with the deep voice I had been enjoying all week.

Upon my arrival, he was still in his work clothes but complimented my teal maxi dress and said he was on his way to change into something more appropriate. That something more appropriate turned out to be sweatpants and a t-shirt. *Hmmm, Lies.* While I was driving us to the local ice cream parlor, I could feel some heavy scrutiny to my right – that discomfort you get when you can literally FEEL someone's eyes on you. When I turned to acknowledge this gaze, I was met with a full frontal face staring at me with wide eyes. *Damn, this is creepy!* He told me he had never seen a woman more beautiful. *Eh, more lies.*

Despite the oddly muggy day, it was still autumn, so the parlor was closed. We decided upon pizza instead, which was perfect because I was famished and was wondering what dinner would be! We learned a little more about each other until a piping hot pepperoni pizza arrived at the table. As the self-proclaimed Queen of the Germophobes, I excused myself from the table to wash my hands. While I gave them a full surgical scrub, I thought about the long day I'd had, how hungry I was, and how I couldn't wait to assault that pizza!

I arrived back to the table to find this man moving all of the food from the hot pan into to-go boxes, touching everything with his filthy-ass, unwashed hands! When I asked what the hell was happening here because I was ready to eat, he told me, "Well I gotta get back to town. I got a 7:00 curfew. I'm on parole."

Shit! There goes my face again! Oh, word? When did he plan on telling *me* this? Because it damn sure didn't come up during the nearly two weeks' worth of phone conversations we'd had. Twenty-three years spent in prison. It's one thing to date a man who got out, has been out for a while, and got his life together. But trying to date someone fresh out with all the extra rules and regulations? It's not for me.

It was 6:40 when he started packing up *my* dinner, and he was forty-two minutes from the city. He was definitely going to be late but I was too ravenous to care. He did that creepy staring thing again all the way from the pizza place to his job where I left him and planned to never see him again. Oh, *and* he had the nerve to take the box with the most slices of pizza in it!

What's that saying? Make a plan, hear God laugh? One day, I was driving through town and a silver SUV was following me and honking incessantly for me to pull over. So like an entire idiot, I did just that. It was *his* ass! He said he'd been trying to call me. *I know, I blocked your calls after the first fifteen in a row. And your messages after the first seven, unanswered.* I need a man without a curfew! Like damn, I'm not even off work until 5:00 so what happens when my good lovin' lasts longer than 7:00?

"Y'all look, I told him I was talking to someone new and I got the hell out of there. I dipped and weaved to make sure he wasn't following me though."

My girls spend the next seven minutes or so cracking jokes about how his sweatpants were "appropriate attire" because he needed to cover his ankle monitor. *I can't stand these heifers.*

♀ ♂ ♀ ♂

ONE WEEK LEFT

"Knock, knock, mamas!!"

Blaire enters my apartment with her table, essential oils, and the hands of heaven every Tuesday for my therapeutic massage. This has been a regularly scheduled event for the past nine years and at current massage rates, I'm certain I have paid off her Honda. She sets up in the middle of the living room which used to be relaxing when my neighbor was an 88-year-old woman, but now with Chaos and Horror living next door... Damn, those probably aren't the children's names.

Expertly running her fingers through my hair and giving my scalp the deep manipulation that she knows I love so much, we giggle and catch up on the events from the previous week. Blaire is a random kind of introvert. She doesn't like people but is in a profession that dictates being pleasant to them. She doesn't care to talk to them but has such a funny and enjoyable presence that makes people want to talk to *her*. She can't stand the stupidity of men but also can't wait to exchange kinky, erotic stories about them with me. She is one giant contradiction that makes me laugh, which is counterproductive to the relaxation I'm supposed to be receiving right now.

"So one more week here! I'm so proud of you for buying your first home! Do you have a spot for me?"

"Damn right!" I've been trying to get Blaire to marry me for years now. Not really, just live with me a little and massage me whenever I want. Be at my beck and call and I will take care of the bills. She's not feeling that arrangement though. Regardless, I have already decided to turn the finished basement into a haven for my weekly indulgence.

Eventually, the talking fades as I begin to relax and fall asleep from Blaire's muscular magic. Just as I am about to drift off, she jumps!

Breathing heavily, "What was *that*!?"

"Just a picture falling off the wall upstairs. It's probably broken."

"Oh my *gosh*! That's insane! How are you so *chill* right now!? I would be *pissed*!"

Of course she would be, her whole place looks like a Pier One showroom. In her house that 4x6 frame would've cost $84. I paid at most $3.99 for mine at the dollar store. At this point, the neighbor's two kids along with the three kids of her trash-ass friend around the corner are running, screaming, jumping, and banging with zero consideration for the fact that this is apartment living. No home training. Blaire and I watch as the lit Yankee Candle, scenting the room of Autumn in the Park, slides across the table as a result of the vibrations coming from the adjoining apartment. She has had the pleasure of experiencing some of the milder noises while massaging me in the past, but it's never been this bad. And it's about to go from bad to worse!

Remember their fight because her baby daddy was "texting some bitch in his car?" Remember how we thought maybe the "bitch" was the angry gonorrhea girl? Well, it's worse than we thought! The "bitch" from the text messages is the same bitch that is currently in my neighbor's kitchen! As frustrated as I am by her, she is definitely on a much higher level, appearance-wise, than her busted friend with the stringy hair and crystal-methed-up teeth. All of their children are playing upstairs together and she's about to find out her friend has been playing with her man. In someone's defense, he's been playing with many people so does it matter much at this point?

I'm in the middle of a calf massage so I'm not sure how it all happened but when the screaming started, my massage stopped. *Um excuse me, I'm paying for this. I'mma need you to listen and rub at the same time. Thank you.* Blaire is standing there wide-eyed, focused on the argument at hand, straining to listen. The cat is still chill because he's accustomed to the anarchy so he changes positions and goes back to sleep. Blaire tries to keep massaging but it's beginning to suffer because her focus is simply too divided. But then we hear the friend scream, "Well I only fucked him a little bit!" Then something was thrown that sounded like it shattered everywhere!

Oh HELLLL Naw! I jump off that table naked as the day I was born, wrapped in only the sheet that was covering me, and bolt over to the wall with Blaire. Like two of the nosiest people alive, our ears are pressed against that wall absorbing ALL of the spilled tea from next door! We are barely breathing because it would make too much noise and we might miss something.

When he starts denying it and telling his girl that he would never have sex with her friend because her mouth is all tore up, I was thinking, *lies.* I sit out on that patio set every night in the dark and watch him come down the back way, down the hill and go to that girl's apartment. And while he's not lying about that dental situation, either that toothless mouth must "do what it do" or he's just hittin' it from the back so he doesn't have to look at her, because he's made repeated visits. Had my neighbor kindly acknowledged my request to move her bed, maybe I would've notified her that her dude was screwing that inbred, stray dog-looking trash bucket. But that's none of my business.

We can hear crying children descending the neighboring stairs while the adults are continuing to violently and hurtfully argue with one another. It really is sad to think about because none of the children should be exposed to that kind of turmoil. Blaire and I then run over to the kitchen window and blatantly peer through the blinds to see what happens outside. We watch in shock as he accompanies the friend with the tore up mouth and her children to her apartment. The door closes and the porchlight turns off – guess he's staying with *her* for the night. After the way he insulted her, I can't believe she would let him!

I'm so confused.

♀ ♂ ♀ ♂

ONE NIGHT LEFT

Stepping out of a late shower to de-funk from all of the packing, my phone lights up with Brie's beautiful cocoa face and grey eyes. She doesn't usually call this late.

"Sooo heyyyy," she says in a seedy, slow manner.

Oh damn. I know what that means. She's about to say something crazy and wildly inappropriate. My sister does the same thing. She starts out a greeting a certain way and I know it's about to be some shit.

"I can *hear* the petty in your voice. Just say it. What is it?"

"So look. I know you are *not* on the vengeful shit, *but* what I'mma need you to do is woman up and call D. He needs to come over there and help you wake up the neighbor so *she* knows how it feels before you move out tomorrow!" *I'm intrigued.* "Somma that extra late night bangin', smackin', screamin', gruntin', all 'at! Make *her* shit fall off the walls for a change – provided she even has anything worth damaging…"

Preach, sis! "Except you know he and I don't have actual sex. He just likes to have a midnight snack, a li'l tasty taste."

"Ok well turn that li'l goodie basket into a whole damn midnight buffet and wake that bitch outta her sleep with YOUR special love melodies and all that freaky BDSM shit that y'all do! And I wanna hear about it in the morning!"

With a heavy sigh, "It's my snack box, bitch." I mutter into an empty phone.

Brie is right, though. I try to be a respectful neighbor but that tart has made my last year here miserable. After finding out her man was cheating with Lady Hoof-In-Mouth, she put all of his belongings out on the porch in garbage bags two days ago. He hasn't been back to retrieve them, so she likely won't be awake with him. I have never asked Diego to just come over before – he just visits and it happens. I don't even know where to start because I don't just DO this. And what if he's already "indisposed" with someone else? *I need a drink. Ok, put on your big girl panties. Ugh, not really, those aren't sexy – they're cotton. Just text him. But what do I say? Something simple and not desperate. But be normal and nonchalant.*

Renée: Hey.

OMG! That was so dumb! I am too old for this shit! I should just have a husband for these activities already - not out soliciting oral sex for revenge purposes! He's probably not even going to reply and I'm going to have to tell Brie that I did a self-service retaliation. She will be so -

DING DING

Diego: Hey Ma. Whachu doin' up so late?

DING DING

Diego: Need me to come pu'chu to sleep?

Well shit! That was easy! So all this time, all I had to do was say "hey" and a man would come to give me the bombest head I've ever had in my LIFE!?

I feel like these bitches have been keeping secrets from me!

DING DING

Diego: I'm gittin a ride ova. Um bringin' the restraints. An put'cha hair in them 2 braids I like. B there in 25. Leave tha door open

I am positive I dried my entire body after my shower, but my lady undercarriage would totally disagree right now. Something about this muscular, dominant, tattooed man giving me orders just makes me want to follow them even though I'm not a woman who can just be bossed around by a man. But Diego knows how to dominate me without hurting me, and when he *does* punish me, it hurts so good. Sometimes I will intentionally disobey him so he'll bend me over and spank me, but he always rubs after he spanks, then kisses it to make it all better. Then, without fail, it's followed by multiple, skillfully crafted orgasms that usually leave me with leg cramps, blurred vision, and some sort of heart condition. I'm convinced this man is trying to kill me with his tongue and my simple ass keeps coming back for more.

A once beautifully decorated bedroom has been reduced to a bed, a dresser, and a chair. The giant plush area rug has been rolled and is ready to move so there is nothing to absorb all of the uproarious sounds that I'm about to make that are *sure* to awaken the entire neighborhood. I'm moving, so I don't care.

If ever studied, I believe science would show that Diego's tongue stimulates the part of the clitoris that is directly connected to the Broca's area of the brain, which controls language. As a result, said language and vocalizations are almost always unintelligible, incomprehensible, and exceedingly loud! She will hear what I've been hearing for the past year because she was too cheap to go buy a damn rug herself! And I am feeling particularly horny and dramatic tonight. I may just quote Shakespeare... or Tyler Perry. Hallelujuerrrrr!! Whatever moves me!

I can hear Diego ascending my stairs toward the empty bedroom. He leans in the doorway, taking me in with his intense hazel eyes like he's going to devour me. Oh, he will. He licks his full, soft lips, then his sly smirk turns into the beautiful smile that he rarely displays. He's probably smiling because I'm wearing his preferred attire – nothing but two pigtails and a Tiffany necklace. Do I feel comfortable? Hell no. This man's body is chiseled caramel perfection which makes me and my tummy pudge & dimply thighs feel like goop, but he has never looked at me that way so that *should* reassure me. It doesn't.

As he gazes around the empty room, Diego allows the restraints to fall from his grasp, loudly clattering onto the floor. "There ain't nothin' ta tie you to in here, Ma. Looks like I'mma have ta restrain you myself," he says with his thick Puerto Rican accent.

"Against this wall, por favor?" Yes, the wall I share with my neighbor.

"It's late. Ya know you get kinda loud when... Ya know..." He raises an eyebrow.

Oh, I know. What I also know is when Diego turns his ball cap around, it's about to go down – HE'S about to go down. He never takes it off – today is the Steeler's cap. I can only assume that means that the Steelers and I are going to end up with the same number of climactic events. That's six for you non-football fans – but if he has it his way, I'll have many more. I don't know how many licks it's taking to get to the center of this tootsie pop but I am slamming and banging every part of my thick, convulsing body against this wall over and over and over again while viciously, violently screaming the song of my multi-orgasmic people. Diego and I revel in the fact that we can hear her next door so pissed off banging on the wall and yelling for me to "SHUT UUPP!!"

Sounds familiar. I feel vindicated and satiated. Brie will be so proud.

Add to my TO-DO list: Not a *damn* thing! Payback feels *so* good - literally

CHAPTER 6
movin' on up

What a way to wake up on moving day! There is a generous, sexy man in my bed telling me he wants to devour me for breakfast. Who am I to tell him to dine elsewhere? That would just be selfish. So bon appetit! Or as I would say to him in Spanish, Buen provecho! But I fear that if he gives me some new lower extremity disorder from the additional stimulation, I'll be no good for the move later. I'm barely functional from last night! So I make a diligent effort to decline and physically stop him, but his dominance overpowers me, as usual, and he raids the snack box anyway.

"Just one and I'll stop," he mumbles flirtatiously.

Liar. Giving just one orgasm is against his entire belief system. After a few rounds with Diego that now have me damn near fluent en Español, I realize I have lost all track of the morning and my mother, my sister, my college friend, and her husband will all be here shortly! Fortunately, my sister is never on time – not for her birth, not for her wedding, nada.

Diego gets dressed and throws on his coat, but leaves it open so his tight Under Armor shirt puts his beautiful midsection on full display for the neighborhood. I'm wearing only a button-down men's shirt, confident that once I see him out, I will be able to hurry and shower before the arrival of my moving assistants. He kisses me goodbye, which lingers a little longer than it should, but only because his lips are so damn soft and touched by the angels. And he always gives my ass a firm squeeze and a smack, which turns me on even more.

I open the door to find that it has warmed up and the snow has turned to slush on this early December day. My mother, Regina, with an annoyed look on her face, is standing on the porch with Desirée and Shawn like they have been there for a little while. Diego exits, holding red and black leather restraints, smirking at everyone, and making no effort to hide the naughty.

"Heyyyy Mama Gina," he says to my mother. Diego and I have known each other for years and my mother thinks he's adorable – even sexy, as disturbing as that is.

"Heyyy D. You know you need to button up! It's chilly out here," she says as she hugs him. I want to throw up in my mouth because it would be great if she would wipe the look of desire off of her face, especially considering where he just had HIS. And never mind that he is hugging my mother while holding the sexual apparatus.

Desirée is shaking her head watching all of this happen but can't help but sneak a peek at the rippling abs on display – she's married, not comatose! Besides, it doesn't matter where you get your appetite, as long as you eat at home, right?

Diego leaves and I'm standing in the entryway in my barely buttoned shirt with nothing beneath. As the breeze blows over me, they all stare at me in silence.

"So thanks for coming guys," I say excitedly.

Silence and stares.

"You weren't out here long, were you?"

Crickets, tumbleweed, and frowns.

"So you heard all that?"

As they begin to finally enter the apartment, my mother purses her lips, "Mmmm hmmm, we heard your li'l naaasty butt."

I gasp in embarrassment as she walks by me. Then Desirée walks in and with her thick island accent says, "You lef' tha bed'rum window cracked. Ever'body heard you."

I drop my forehead into my hand, thank Heavens I'm moving today! Shawn walks past laughing, "But your Spanish is coming along nicely. I understood most of it."

Desirée softly punches him and laughs because Shawn stays with jokes, always clowning somebody.

"Oh and uh… yeah, I ain't touching those sheets. That's all you," he laughs.

While they begin packing up the remainder of the downstairs, I run upstairs to "throw some water" as my mom would say, and get dressed. I quickly snatch all of the linens and the protective pad off the master bedroom mattress so I don't have to hear Shawn's mouth. Otherwise, he will go on for days.

Desirée joins me upstairs to reprimand me, "Now you know betta than ta have tha person who always late bringin' tha mos' important thing – tha truck!?"

She's right. Des is always #facts. And they tend to spill out of her mouth in whatever manner she sees fit. Tact? Who needs it? She's about telling all of it like it is. And when she's upset, her accent gets really thick and you just have to try to catch what words you can! When we first met in undergrad, she was so quiet and shy… and mean! I have always been so boisterous and outgoing so she just seemed weirdly antisocial to me. My mother told me I had to be nice to her, so I was, and when she finally came out of her shell, she's been crazy cool ever since with her snappy wit and a side eye that will make you question everything you ever did wrong in your life. I knew she was about to be one of the true homies when I called her after a bad date and she said in her thick island accent, "Who me got ta go put a curse on?"

Yasss!! Because every woman needs a stable of passionate bitches on hand. The ones you call for an alibi. The ones you call to bring shovels. The ones you call when there's about to be an ass-whoopin'. They all know who they are and are familiar with their roles. And now I have one on my team who handles the curses. On their teams, I'm more of the alibi and shovels chick. They know better than to call me to be fighting somebody – my hair is entirely too long for that mess.

Desirée is in the master closet boxing the last of a few miscellaneous items. I feel like a parent; when they hear certain sounds or don't hear anything at all and know one of the children is getting into something they shouldn't be. Pretty sure Des has found my Holy Grail – a wooden, hand-crafted box of eclectic... toys.

"Renée? Wha's thisss?" she slowly shouts to me, accent in full force.

"If it came out of that little brown box and you have to ask what it is, then you probably shouldn't be touching it!" I shout back from the guestroom.

"Right, so I'mma go wash me hands now." On her way to the bathroom, she passes Shawn, who is making his way upstairs to start moving the larger items. She whispers, "Babe, we gotta get us somma wha's in dat box!" She winks and pats him on the bum.

"What box?" he asks, intrigued as he watches her walk away. "*Bae*, what box!?"

So glad I can be an inspiration to my friends, meanwhile I haven't used the contents of my toy chest in what feels like ages - even though I have the batteries now. I hope to change that in the new house – if I can ever find a functional man who isn't afraid of commitment and ball gags.

As we begin to move the mattress downstairs, I hear Shawn whisper to Des, "Bae, this ain't the mattress she paid $666 for, is it? You know that's the mark of The Beast!"

"Yup, dis tha devil bed. Na worry I got some holy water out inna car, we gon be fine. We gon spray it down when we get ta the new house. Us too."

"Yo. You know if she conceives on this thing, she gon have Rosemary's baby, right? DAMIAANNNN!!" They are laughing hysterically while trying not to drop Satan's mattress down the thirteen stairs.

"I'M RIGHT HERE, GUYS! I CAN HEAR YOU!" I yell at them.

Still cracking up, they don't care. By the time we reach the bottom of the stairs, we can hear a commotion outside. Sounds like baby daddy has returned to find his belongings have been put out in melted, snow-covered garbage bags. Des is thrilled to experience this dramatic affair first-hand, as she has only ever heard the stories over the phone – and they sound too farfetched to believe.

"Wow, dis is ridiculous! Ya can hear every word they sayin'! These walls!"

"I know! It's constant. I've filed complaints. I've called the cops. No one cares."

But I guess when you're in public housing, the general perception is that we all behave like animals. Not true. And not all housing projects are created equally. This is not the stereotypical, rundown, income-based housing that you see in the urban movies, though some of my neighboring tenants may behave like it. This complex is situated in a fairly well-maintained part of town and the racial breakdown skews toward more Caucasian residents. Regardless, there is still a stigma associated with living in the projects that I felt as a child, from being referred to as "one of those project children" by my fourth-grade teacher, to being judged in doctors' offices as an adult. Being talked down to based on my address, but not realizing that when I receive just one more degree, we will call each *other* "Dr." So really, I should *thank* my trashy neighbor, without whom I would likely still be in this same apartment where I've spent my entire life.

The fighting continues while we head back upstairs to pack up and wait for my tardy sister to arrive with the U-Haul truck. Everyone is shocked when the house phone rings because we all just assumed that someone had already disconnected and packed it. After a few minutes, I realize we can hear a one-sided conversation from my mother, who I guess answered the phone. Though she occasionally receives calls here when people know she's visiting, they're far and few between. *Whatever, just keep packing.*

Unbeknownst to us, she is downstairs having a conversation with a man she doesn't know, who called for *me*. Midway through the conversation, she realizes she has no clue who this man is and that the call isn't for her and comes up to discreetly ask if this call should be for me. Of course, because he called *my* house, but my hands are full so I can't take the call – I didn't want to anyway because that guy never shuts up! I once put the phone down, went to the bathroom, washed my hands, got an apple, came back to the phone, and he was still talking! She proceeds to humor him for an additional few minutes without telling him that it wasn't *me* who he was talking to! Who does that!? Unsure of how to get him off the phone, she finally tells him that he's breaking up and to call back later and then hangs up on him!!

Des and I are cracking up because Mother's facial expressions rival mine in terms of control. So now I'll have to return this man's call and tell him he was on the phone with my mama and that she now knows all of his business.

Baby daddy finally takes his garbage bags to his car parked up on the hill – ya know, where he parks when he's going to have sex with his girlfriend's friend with the mouth issues. You still with me here? I know it's a mess – welcome to my world.

"Ooooh, he really gon take tha milk AN' tha TV!?" Des looks to me for verification like I'm somehow involved in this hot mess of a lover's spat. "OOOH! Not tha Christmas tree! Wha' 'bout them babies!?"

Look, he said he bought that tree with *his* money so it's his! She's kicking him out so he's taking his tree! And yes, we are packing and intently listening as they argue about him leaving with that tree. The two children are crying while we can only imagine he's removing the ornaments from that spruce, Grinch-style.

"Yo! Dude really left wit' this tree! Like, he for real just took a Christmas tree from his kid!" Shawn exclaimed.

Everyone in my apartment is shocked as they watch him glide down the street with the tree propped up on his left shoulder, lights dangling off of it... remaining ornaments falling off... I, of course, am the only one not shocked because I have been witness to this psychotic back and forth for the past year and a half. Yeah, of course he took the tree. Probably taking it up and around the corner to her friend's house but they'll be back together next week. He will apologize, buy her a new tree, then get her pregnant again. But the next time he gives someone chlamydia or anything else, I won't be here to hear about it, and for that, I am blessed and highly favored.

My sister Neka finally arrives and, as usual, makes a grand entrance with her loud and ultra-foul mouth. She's huffing in exasperation, "What the FUCK! Y'all *know* I don't like to drive! Comin' up this hill, I almost hit a man who was runnin' wit' a damn *tree*! Lights and tinsel 'n shit fallin' all off like he STOLE 'at bitch!" She pauses to read the room to see if her assessment of the events is accurate. No one looks surprised so she continues, "WHAT. They stealin' TREES UP HERE NOW!?"

The situation itself wasn't funny but her response to it was hilarious because yes, that man just stole his children's Christmas tree back to take to his other chick. If that ain't some ratchet, hood mess, I don't know what is. So we all look at each other and nod, like, yeah that's pretty much what happened.

"Oh. Ok. Well as long as we're *clear*! I got a pic so I'm postin' this shit on my Instagram."

♀ ♂ ♀ ♂

We arrive at my new home, conveniently only six blocks away from the apartment. I now live on a corner lot connected to no one! Peace and solitude are mine at last! I was so excited when my mom came into town to see the house and immediately loved it as much as I did. As soon as she walked in, she said it felt like home. She and I have always shared a brain - those were my sentiments exactly! I'm thrilled that my sister and friends like the house as well. I have some things to handle yet, like the landscaping needs prayer and I'm still trying to figure out who fought the curb outside and won because it's a mess. Overall, the house doesn't really need any work and everything I plan to do is a personal, aesthetic choice.

Neka immediately runs up onto my porch, leans her thick upper body over the ledge, and begins to twerk screaming, "Ayyyy sis! I know you bout ta git it poppin' out here! This porch is nice! An' you ain't got no neighbors *either*!?"

Although the house directly next door is still vacant, the rest of my neighbors are probably thinking, great, there goes the neighborhood. They will be relieved to know that Neka and I are sisters but we are as different as night and day. Though only a few years apart, we share the same father but weren't raised in the same home, except for summers at Nana's house. She was raised in the inner city and exposed to life way sooner than I was out in the backward suburbs. I remember her explaining to *me* what birth control was. Lord knows my mother wasn't doing that – she didn't even tell me about my period. I had to find out about *that* at summer camp when it surprised me for the first time. Lesson learned. Have questions? Ask my baby sister – the wild child to my clueless naïveté. Remember that stable of bitches? Neka is definitely the cuss you out/ass-whoopin' bitch. I can't call her for the alibi though because she likes to smoke – she might forget the damn story.

Desirée walks up onto the porch and says to Neka, "Child. You na see that church ova der? God is watchin' you." Then spritzes her in the face with a loose mist of the aforementioned bottle of Holy Water, which I'm convinced is nothing but some Evian. I could be wrong but I'm not trying to find out. I don't need those problems.

As wicked as Desi's side-eye is, my sister's is worse. With the angry almond shape of her dark, sexy eyes, which directly contrast her very fair skin, comes a string of curse words so artfully assembled that you don't know if you should feel insulted or try to remember it so you can go copyright it. But Neka holds her tongue since she knows Desirée is an ordained minister and it's in poor taste to fight a pastor in front of a church. That's like a first-class, one-way ticket to Hell.

"So ya certainly got enough room ta add some children – four bedrooms is a lot for jus' you," Desi says while we organize room by room.

"It ain't about to be just her, girl. That fool she just went out with 'bout to bring *allll* them babies up in here!! My math is bad, what is that? Three kids per room?" Neka laughs.

Yes. I had a date the other night with a guy who told me he had nine kids under twelve years old - but that he takes care of all of his kids. Sir, given your current menial profession, I refuse to believe you're taking care of nine children in any sort of functional manner. And I have a great many questions to which I require answers: How many baby mamas is that? What the hell were you doing with your "man member" that you have that many kids that close in age? Eww. What kind of custody situation do you think is happening here? Because if you think all these kids are coming to MY house every other weekend and on Wednesdays, you're out of your whole damn mind!

"I think I may have contracted syphilis telling that story! Oh, but FYI, he still wants to have a baby with *me*! Then there was the other guy who didn't have *any* kids. He said he went on The Maury Povich Show and was told he was *not* the father. Said he didn't believe Maury and wanted a second opinion so he went on The Steve Wilkos Show where he was also told he wasn't the father. So he wants a baby now too. Why, so you can drag my ass on national television to question its paternity? No thanks! I'm not having a baby with either of y'all!"

Everyone in this house is dying laughing because a paternity test is *not* an opinion and only I could meet two men on opposite ends of the spectrum and find they both be completely unstable.

"Well sis, I did notice them freaky hooks comin' out the ceiling in the finished attic… sooo… if you do decide to call one of them for some baby makin', there's this website with some interestin' lookin' swings…"

"Ok. First of all, No. Secondly, I noticed those too and I already asked the home inspector if he thought they could support my weight. No judgment, please. He said he wouldn't suggest it if I wanted to keep my roof. So I don't think the previous owner had them installed for that purpose, pervert."

Add to my TO-DO list: Buy a stud finder and re-locate those attic sex hooks

CHAPTER 7
shit my mom says

Christmas in the new house has been wonderful with Mom back in town, though I can't seem to figure this woman *out*! She's only here for one week, but the two of us had to make multiple trips to the car to get all of her luggage. My foyer looks like she's here for the damn month! I take her coat to hang and then give her a huge hug only to notice that she feels *so* much fluffier than usual.

"Why are you wearing so many *clothes*!? Like for real, it's not *that* cold."

"Cuz I couldn't fit 'em in either of the three suitcases so I wore 'em all."

"OMG, you are here for *one* week! ONE! You don't need this many clothes! I don't have *room* for you to have this many clothes here!"

"You know I need options."

I can't with her. "I'm not helping you unpack this mess. You don't need options, you need therapy."

She spends the next two hours unpacking the carful of luggage she hauled across the state, then inevitably conks out across the bed, on top of the covers, of course with the television and all of my lights on. I mean, who needs to conserve electricity when I just bought a house? The room is still in total disarray and I often find myself so confused because when my mother leaves my home, I find the *weirdest* stuff in my guest room. Last time, I found a tampon & bubbles! Like, WTF!? Mama is in menopause... and the bubbles? Well, I just have no words.

I'm awakened in the middle of the night, but it's not by sex this time for a change. It's an oddly refreshing feeling that doesn't last long when I realize someone is frantically banging on my screen door. I've lived here less than a month and already some foolishness is happening! Fortunately, mama is here, otherwise, I would've been totally freaked out alone in this huge house with someone outside assaulting my entrance. I groggily stumble out of bed and open the bedroom door to find my mother already standing at the upstairs railing peeking down the stairs toward the main entry. So I peek around as well. The banging persists and we continue to stand staring at each other like neither of us hears a thing. It's the middle of the damn night! In every slasher film ever made, Black people are the first to die in these scenarios. So we know to continue to stand frozen like baby deer until it stops because our "horror movie heritage" dictates that we stay put. Once the banging ends, mama shoots me an inquisitive look that says, are you gonna go check that out?

"Are you crazy? *I'm* not goin' down there! You're the parent, *you* go first!"

"It's *your* house!"

"Yes, but you're *old*, you've lived your life!" We both quietly giggle then head down the steps together with me carrying the mini Louisville Slugger Mama gave me, and she, armed with the hatchet that I've always kept at the top of the stairs in my apartment. Please don't ask why, because even I don't know.

Fortunately, whoever decided to lose it on my porch is now long gone. We breathe sighs of relief as we see that all the person left was a giant handprint on my glass door. Unbeknownst to me, I now live directly in front of the only apartment complex in the area that has been nicknamed the domestic disturbance apartments. Go figure – here we go again with the drama! At least I'm not connected to it this time.

Mama follows me back upstairs into my room to finish our conversation since we're now both wide awake at 2 a.m.

DING DING

VIDEO MESSAGE

"Who's texting *you* this late?"

"No clue, but they should know better." I open it and shriek at full volume, "OMG!"

My mother nosily approaches and looks over my shoulder to see a dark chocolate man, who I have never *met*, by the way, fully and openly stroking his man monster. He and I have been having phone conversations but nothing that would suggest that this should be the next step in our courtship. I don't even know his last name, but I might be about to find out his sperm count! He is staring dead into the camera, breathing heavily looking straight at us – well me. Mama wasn't supposed to be there. I was so shocked that it took me a minute to realize what we were watching and that this should *not* constitute mother/daughter bonding time! So I immediately slam the phone face down, but since I didn't turn it off, we could hear him very vocally "finishing." Then silence. From all parties. Then my dear, sweet mother looks at me and says, "Soooo you wanna send that to me?"

"MOM!! EWWW!!!!" And I run out of my <u>own</u> bedroom shaking my entire body like I'm covered in spiders – or covered in the thought of my ancient ass mother having sex. Both are kind of bothersome and unpleasant to picture.

"What?" she asks. "I'm old, I'm not dead!"

♀ ♂ ♀ ♂

With Mama's help, within three days, we managed to get everything organized and looking like I have hosted Christmas here for years. We put up a tree and decorated for the holidays to blend in with the festive feel of the rest of the block. As warped as she is, my mother, Regina, is truly the best and I am so lucky to have her. We have an oddly open relationship where we can tell each other anything. Though given her age, there are a great many things that I no longer care to hear. She is my only actual parent, as my paternal unit bought me a trumpet in grade school and thought his responsibilities were complete. He showed up for all of the large events, presumably to silently brag that his kid was the trumpet soloist in the jazz ensemble or that his kid was the only African American inducted into the National Honor Society. He was also quick to brag that his kid graduated college with honors with no books. *Yeah, hey Dad! That's nothing to brag about because most students have parents who help with that*. My mom helped where she could but *he's* the one who had the means to send me off to college with a computer, and instead, elected to do the responsible thing and buy himself a new motorcycle.

I have no doubt that this is where a portion of my dating issues stem from and why my friends call me "picky" all the time. There are several things I shouldn't have to settle for in a relationship, and all of the selfish actions that remind me of my paternal unit top the list. In addition to his self-centered behavior, he wasn't affectionate, never expressed feelings or emotions, couldn't communicate effectively, rarely spent quality time, serial dated because he couldn't stay faithful to one woman, and smoked enough weed to choke a horse. Most importantly, he never said "I love you" – only "I love you too." There is a *huge* difference. As an experiment, I stopped saying it to see if he would ever initiate it and I never heard "I love you" from him again. So naturally, when a man comes along with similar attributes, he is not a desirable candidate to me, even though he appears to have his life together otherwise. Not wanting to date the younger version of a person who has caused so much damage in my life isn't picky, it's smart. But either way, I will end up needing therapy for this. Fortunately, my mother was there for me in all the ways he wasn't. Though she couldn't afford that college computer, she tried to spend as much time with me as she could when I was away at school in Cleveland. I'm certain it's just because her hot tail liked ogling all the basketball players though.

It's always been just the two of us, but over the years, somehow my kind-hearted mother has acquired several additional children. It would always garner peculiar looks from strangers in the 90's when two Caucasian girls would run up to a clearly African American woman and scream, "Hey Mommmm!!" and shower her with hugs. But Liza and Julia are my sisters and we've been friends since kindergarten and third grade, respectively. I also call their mothers "Mom." Their daughters are my nieces and I dare someone to say otherwise. I show up at soccer games cheering like an absolute fool for an adorable blonde-haired, grey-eyed bolt of lightning in cleats. People look at me and I can only imagine them wondering, "What child does this crazy woman belong to? There are no Black children on this field." *Look. I'm "Auntee" and I'm here for the child who just ran over* yours. *Please have a seat.*

"I need to run and get you some Arm & Hammer for your fridge," Mom yells from the kitchen.

"Why?"

"It smells like chicken in here. You can't just be having the girls over and the fridge be smellin' all suspect!"

"Really, Regina? We *just* air-fried a whole *farm* of chickens yesterday, then put it *all* in the fridge. I would be worried if it *didn't* smell like chicken."

"Oh... yeah... We did... Well, I *guess* it's ok then."

Swear my mother is six feet of cluelessness and naïveté most days, but she makes everyone who interacts with her laugh, so I guess it's ok.

The annual gift exchange with Julia and Liza takes place at one of our homes where we act like giant children eating, laughing, joking, opening gifts and just catching up on each other's lives. This year it's happening at my new digs.

Our day usually begins with a shopping excursion at one of the local malls for Jules because she is the overall size of a sixth grader but curvy and shaped like a grown-ass woman. Her 4' 10" frame walking through the mall with me towering easily a foot taller often makes it look like I'm babysitting. The wavy, reddish-brunette hair, glasses, and Mickey Mouse t-shirt don't help her to look any older. Despite her petite size, she has a highly secretive position doing some sort of job that none of us really know about, but if we ask too many questions, we're convinced she'll have to kill us. So I just shop with her and try to dress her like an actual adult while she engages in her clandestine occupation. Our visits to Victoria's Secret are always a delight, as it looks like I'm about to sell a young girl into the sex trade. I have to say things like, "Oh your *husband* will love that!" so I don't look like some creepy lady pimp.

So remember my stable of passionate bitches? Well, I have two, and let's just say they don't exactly intermingle in terms of roles. I can't call this stable to help with the ass-whoopin' because they're both too damn small, though Julia would absolutely overnight me a shovel. And it would be a top-of-the-line, high-tech one too; one that has GPS and Bluetooth but doesn't leave prints! But this is my stable of bitches who I call about my creditworthiness, finances, net worth, retirement plan, savings, etc... Julia won't even pay her bills early because she doesn't want to lose interest on the money being removed from the account. And had it not been for watching Liza and her family's fiscal operations, I would've never been able to walk into a real estate office and leave with six figures in financing with no work to do on my credit. That was Liza. So to this day, I'm still not sure why she knocks on my door; bitch come *in*! *We* live here.

But as usual, there's a knock anyway, and my mom is quick to open the door for Liza, greeting her with tons of hugs and kisses. She enters and removes her coat to get comfy in her charcoal leggings that silhouette her amazing legs, and an oversized college hoodie. I light the fireplace for the first time and it looks just as delightful as it feels. Liza quickly hops in front of it to warm up and her golden hair and clear grey eyes sparkle in the flickers. *Sigh, I'm supposed to be making love in front of this thing, not sitting around it with a horde of womenfolk.* But I'm astonished by how much heat emanates from such a small area – we might just combust trying to get nasty in front of this thing!

This year, I've planned a crafty scavenger hunt for the ladies to change things up a bit – gonna make them work for it! After making their way through all four levels of the new house and quickly mastering all of the clues to locate their gifts, they finally make it to the last clue which reads:

OMG, you're super smart
And good at all your looking,
So your gift is in the area
Where I rarely do my cooking

"To the BEDROOM!!!" Julia shouts and takes off. Clearly in agreement, Liza quickly follows her, sprinting two flights from the basement to my master suite where they begin to search for the gifts.

I yell for them to wait but they are completely convinced that they have the correct answer to this clue as they ignore my screams. When I finally make it to the bedroom, completely out of breath, I ask with a slight attitude, "Yo! Skanks! *Why* are you in this room!?"

Julia offers a look of confusion, "Well, you said the room that you rarely do your cooking. Ain't nothing cookin' in *here*!" Liza snickers and continues to search under the bed, trying not to laugh.

"Woww, everybody got jokes today! *Wrong. Room.*"

As they dejectedly exit the bedroom, Liza whispers to Julia, "Must be the kitchen then because her potato salad is just sadness." Julia agrees and they stroll to the kitchen where they find the last of their gifts inside the air fryer.

After opening gifts, I tell them about my pizza and parolee date and they both laugh and agree that it sounds like a new show on TLC. Julia tells me that in her area of Virginia, there is so much diversity and that there are chocolate men everywhere - educated, career-minded men just for me and that I would definitely find a suitable candidate there. I politely remind them of the other men who were just as educated and focused from outside of the Pittsburgh area.

Shall we discuss Maxwell, who attended college with me in Cleveland? He messaged me on the dating app and I remembered him from his profile pictures. I did find it odd though, that *all* of the photos seemed to be from those college years. We chatted on the phone for a few weeks during which time I inquired as to how similar he looked to his photos. He confirmed that since college was only a few years ago, he still looked the same. Wonderful, because he was a very handsome man with a great smile.

He drove in from Ohio to spend the weekend so we could hang out and get to know each other better. I offered to meet him at the exit to avoid any confusion with the directions, as they could be a little tricky. When I pulled my car up to his, driver side to driver side like the police do it, I noticed that he was a little fuller in the face than his photos suggested, but it didn't seem like anything too drastic.

Once we pulled up to my apartment, Maxwell popped his trunk, so I asked if there was anything I could help him unload. Still in his car gathering items, he simply said that his stuff was in the back. So I looked into the trunk and noticed some car supplies, a spare tire, a giant bottle of window washer fluid, and a laundry basket. No luggage. So I hollered up to him and asked if he forgot to bring his luggage and he confirmed that it was back there. Maybe it's behind his laundry? So I took a peek – nope, nothing. So I was thinking to myself, *damn this dude is about to be here with no draw's.* He finally got out of his car and I should've known something was about to go ghastly awry when the entire driver's side lifted and sat level once he was out. He came around to the trunk and I promise he was 173.56 lbs. *heavier* than he was in *any* of those photos! *Is this the same man who told me he looked the same as in his photos? Is he the same person who said college wasn't that long ago? I gained a few pounds since undergrad but not a few PEOPLE!* Why can't these men simply be honest and not out here catfishing? Had he just been up front, I would've known what to expect, thus eliminating that element of surprise.

So he reached into the trunk and pointed out his travel items – the laundry basket of what I thought were just dirty clothes. *You didn't feel compelled to run to Walmart right quick and purchase a bag? Or borrow your son's sports duffel? Or grab your Nana's suitcase? No? Just gonna throw it into a laundry basket and leave town like the zombies are comin', huh?*

He said he was going to bring his trumpet since we both play. When I asked if it was in the back seat, he simply pulled back a shirt and a pair of undies and there it was. An expensive brass instrument just strewn in with the laundry, unprotected. Meanwhile, my black-silver Bach Stradivarius, affectionately named Lu-Lu, is in her case, wrapped and protected from any and all elements that could potentially harm her.

To make matters worse, he showed up in the middle of summer with only jeans to wear along with an array of Cleveland Browns shirts. Yes, in Pittsburgh, like we aren't bitter rivals. This very large man sweat through all of his clothes the entire time he was here – and he did so in my *guestroom*, as *my* bedding would not have been able to sustain that level of moisture.

And then there was the fella who came in from Michigan. I picked him up at the Greyhound station and he looked just as he did in his photos – tall, light complexion, hazel eyes, cute smile. On that freezing cold January night, we got into the car and I turned up the heat. As we were getting to know one another in person, I began to smell a foul stench that started to permeate the interior of my new car! At first, I thought maybe something was wrong with the car, but it didn't take long to realize it was his breath! So I tilted the car's sunroof to allow some fresh air in – never mind that it was only 22 degrees outside. Naturally, he asked why I opened it so I had to make something up about my core body temperature. I tried to stay quiet the remainder of the ride to my apartment, but he just kept talking and that stench kept eating through my dashboard and sound system! The warranty was *not* going to cover that! Eventually, I ended up cracking the driver's side window, trying my best to angle my face in that direction to inhale air that didn't smell like the deepest crevice of someone's ass.

Upon arriving to my apartment, he asked where he would be sleeping. Oh, right here in this guest room. It has cable and a fully stocked mini fridge.

This man was not about to be up in *my* bed burning through my expensive sheets with that hot dragon-ass breath of his! I spent the whole rest of his visit trying to evade his halitosis, which was exceedingly difficult considering it was winter and the only activities available were all indoors with minimal airflow. I just *knew* I was going to pass out in the theater each time he leaned in with commentary throughout the movie, whispering that death breath all up in my ear. I could feel the wax crawling further into my auditory canal to escape the stench and I know for a *fact* that the earring in that ear *before* the movie was 14kt yellow gold. Now all that's left is just stainless steel after that corrosive ass, landfill-scented air from his mouth ate through it.

Hearing Liza's loud, infectious laugh from in the kitchen makes my mother crack up overhearing these stories again and the girls are still howling along with her, hearing it for the first time.

"What was his name again?" calls my mother.

"I honestly don't even remember his name, just that noxious breath! Oh and Ma, you remember dude with the mint ice cream and the bug!?"

When only Liza and Mom crack up, Liza inquires, "You don't remember that, Jules!?"

Julia is feeling left out of the laughter and is anxious to hear about the summer ice cream date I had with a gentleman whose name I also don't recall. What is unfortunately burned into my memory forever is him ordering mint chocolate chip ice cream, sitting two feet away from me, and still being able to smell the horror show called his mouth over that mint ice cream!

He wanted to walk and eat our cones, which was fine with me since I was deep in prayer that the air would blow that funk in the opposite direction of my delicate nasal sensibilities. But of course, since karma and I had another fight, there was no breeze that day. So as we strolled along and afternoon turned to dusk, a lightning bug landed on my beautifully manicured index finger. Being the random bug weirdo that I am, I held her up to my face a little closer to inspect and say hello. Why did she land on me of all places? Was she injured? Was she even a she? I don't know - I'm not *that* much of a bug weirdo to go find out. So we walked along with this little insect on my finger for a few blocks and I was holding my hand out in front of me in case she wanted to fly away. All of a sudden, I felt this burst of searing, hostile, burning anger on my hand. This man with the septic tank for a throat just thought it would be cute to forcefully blow the lightning bug off of my finger.

Why? She was just chillin'. Wasn't hurtin' a soul. That poor bug probably never found a mate because its butt couldn't light up anymore due to the trauma inflicted by that volatile mouth heat! Also, in my mind, I could feel the flesh deteriorating from my finger and I could *hear* my French manicure develop a German accent.

"That's insane! That poor bug will never be the same," Julia says laughing. "Why don't you just tell these men that they're destroying your entire sinus situation?"

"What for? Plus, do you know how *hard* it is to tell someone their breath is hot? It's only really worth it if you really like him, if you think he is worth dealing with, and if he has the good sense and dental insurance to correct it."

"Truth. Speaking of bad smells, do you smell that?" an always hyper-vigilant Julia asks.

"Oh shit, it's not my breath is it?" I ask jokingly, knowing it better not be as much time as I spend at the dentist – hell I worked for Dornin Dental for four years. We all laugh but pause and focus on our breathing to try to smell what she's smelling. There is definitely something, but we can't quite place what it is.

"I think it's coming from your fireplace maybe?" as Liza walks over to it. "Oh yeah, this is definitely it."

"Did you open the flue?" Julia askes.

What the hell's a flue? My realtor said this is a ventless gas fireplace. Light it and go right? Wrong.

More things people never tell me! Apparently, the previous owners duct-taped the flue shut with no explanation as to why. The house was built in 1928 so I can only assume there is a human *hand* in there or something, but I don't care to untape it right now to find out.

Turns out the fumes are from a heat reaction to the chemicals in the tape so we all go from room to room opening the windows after turning off the fireplace.

"Good thing you were just with *us*. You would've *died* trying to have sex in front of that thing! All that heavy breathing!?" Julia jokes.

Add to my TO-DO list: Throw the whole fireplace away and start over

♀ ♂ ♀ ♂

Other than the dates gone wrong and the house filling with fumes that almost killed us all, tonight was great. Everyone loved their gifts, and Mama got to spend some quality time with her girls, but now it's time to put my mother to bed like a giant child. If left to her own devices, she will fall asleep sitting upright on my couch with all of the downstairs lights on because she gives zero shits about my utility bills. Usually, I can just lure both her and the cat up the stairs with treats.

I enter the guest room, which she likes to refer to as "her room," and ask if she can please put all this hair in a braid before I go to bed. She agrees, positions herself behind me facing the large mirror, and begins to finger through the long, thick tresses.

"Woww, this one's niiice, it feels better than the piece I'm wearing. Why don't you let me borrow this for tomorrow?"

"Regina! This is not a wig; this is *my hair*!"

"WHHAAAAATTTTT!!!! I didn't *know*! It feels so thick and... fake!"

"Seriously!? Don't talk to me for the rest of this trip! *You* are my *mother*! YOU should *know* better!"

"It's a compliment," she says innocently as she completes my braid.

I throw a rubber band on the end and hop into the guest room bed to spend a few additional moments with my mom even though she has totally insulted me. She has the news on, which I don't care for because it's usually something negative. She lies atop the covers beside me.

"It's gonna be 56 degrees tomorrow!? It's winter!"

"I know," I say with deep concern. "The world is coming to an end. I need to get laid, ma."

She returns that concerned look and raises an eyebrow.

"Well hell. *You're* in the wrong damn *bed* then! I can't help you!"

I leave and head to my bedroom laughing because nothing about that woman or our interactions is normal. But I love her so much.

CHAPTER 8
cupid needs punched

B laire is back in the house but without her massage table this time. The surprise for her is that I now have my own, so all she needs to do is show up and rub me – sounds so tawdry. The basement is all set up for her, complete with Himalayan salt lamps and an area to house the sheets, oils, and lotions. Virtually no lighting though, because if it were up to me, she would be massaging me through holes cut in my sweatshirt in pitch blackness while wearing night vision goggles. But she might charge extra for that so I just act like the Motel 6 and leave the light on for her.

"I *know* you found a man to celebrate Valentine's Day with tonight, yes gypsy?"

Of course not! I can only assume she is asking this because she still to this day massages Owen, the guy with whom I spent last V-day. He said he had never received a professional massage so I gave him one of her gift certificates. I'm not the girl who only takes on the holiday of love; I also listen and give relevant gifts in return. I also bought him the electric blanket he wanted, which I had to hear about from my friends because he wasn't my man. They said I spent too much money and probably wouldn't get much in return.

The homegirls all know that among my many issues, I tend to be too giving, even when in non-committed situationships. I give, they take. I give more, and they take more while bringing nothing to the table except a fork to eat everything that I've already provided. This is a common thread in the uneven patchwork of so many of my recent relation/situationships.

So naturally, when Owen was hinting around trying to figure out my preferred flower and suggested coming over to cook me a shrimp dinner, my giving nature kicked into full gear and I spent three figures on this man I had only gone out with twice.

With plastic shopping bags in tow, he entered my apartment looking and smelling as inviting as the dinner that he was about to prepare.

"I got you flowers," he said, beaming with pride. I was so excited because I hadn't received flowers from a man in what felt like decades, especially for Valentine's Day.

Wait, what the hell is THIS!? Owen pulled a miniature rose bush out of a bag. I can barely keep this cat alive and now I have a plant? Kitty usually sits and stares longingly at the refrigerator which tells me that I haven't watered *him* in a while, which means this poor bush has a survival rate of about .26 percent.

What am I supposed to DO with this? I thought he was bringing me actual roses, like the ones with the stems you put in water, and post as an arrangement on social media so it looks like someone gives a crap about you for at least ONE day.

"Hey, there *are* roses on there," he said defensively.

Yes, there were. Tiny roses. On a little bush. So as I attempted to recover from the disappointment of my Day-of-Love "roses," I was setting the table while he prepared a Jamaican shrimp feast for us. I broke out the good dishes and flatware for the occasion. These weighted, solid white, square plates with blunt edges are the reason Americans are overweight. Filling even half of this plate would be vastly overeating, but the food smelled amazing so I was ready to get full.

I brought our plates to the stove so he could load them up and the excitement took over! I'd never had a man come to my home and cook for me before. This was so sweet. He placed a large spoonful of rice, then veggies onto the plate, and then shrimp. My *fave*! Lobster, crab, and shrimp! Any way they can be prepared, I'm all in and ready to eat! This man scooped five shrimp onto my plate. No, no. NO. Not five jumbo, *face and whole body still attached* prawns - five baby, nickel-sized shrimp.

"Where are the *rest*?" I asked with a combination of confusion, frustration, and hanger. These scrawny little things looked like the miniature version of what the adults eventually grow up to be.

"Well, I figured, I get five and you get five. This is all the shrimp I had left."

I need to just invest in a whole face mask because I know I had to have been looking at him like he was seven shades of crazy! You offered to cook a woman a shrimp dinner. BUY MORE SHRIMP! My plates are easily 14" x 14" so those five little shrimp shivering in the corner looked like nothing of significance where an actual meal was concerned. I'm a sturdy chick who likes to eat, so I should've put him out and eaten *all* the shrimp myself! But I didn't. I stewed in hunger and silence and ate my five baby shrimp and a few bites of rice and veggies. I bought a chocolate crème pie for dessert, at which point he had the nerve to stare at me like I was greedy for slicing ¼ of the pie for myself. Look, Chef Boyar-PLEASE GO BUY SOME SHRIMP, I was deprived of actual dinner, I'll be damned if I was going to be deprived of dessert too!

As I washed the dishes, along with the small section of the plates that actually had food on them, I contemplated whether or not to give him the gift card for the massage. I decided, for his effort, to give him the gift of Blaire's hands, but that electric blanket found a home on my couch. As for that poor bush, I came downstairs the next morning to find the cat on top of the dryer eating it. Pitiful little bush never had a chance, so that's what got posted to social media.

Blaire is giggling while we reminisce about poor clueless Owen – a man who would wear multiple pairs of pants at once because... well, we're still not exactly sure why.

"So what's the plan for tonight, Sugarplum?" Blaire always has some sort of pet name for me.

"Nothing tonight, but I'm supposed to meet someone on Friday."

"Oooooh baby," she coos as she tickles me flirtatiously.

"Stopppp!!" I laugh, "It's not officially a Valentine's date, it just happens to be the night we are both available, though I'm sure everyone else will be out celebrating their love. Who's tying *you* up tonight, Miss Nasty?"

"That's 'Your Kinkiness' to you, peasant. Ugh, but no one. Just whatever eye candy Chicago Med, Fire & PD have to offer on my DVR from last week."

"Oh, well any one of *them* can tie *me* up too," I say in jest but also semi-serious.

"Well, you text me and tell me all about the date! You deserve to find someone special. A King who knows to treat his lady like a Queen instead of all these court jesters you keep meeting. Like the guy who bought you that giant dick pop that one year! That thing was *massive*!"

"And remember I sucked the head right OFF of it!?" We both laugh hysterically. So much for a relaxing massage.

She pauses and takes a deep breath and a long sigh, "Man, it's so *quiet* here!"

"*Riiight*!?!?" We laugh, "Don't you *love* it!?"

"Is there a cold cellar down here?"

"I'm not sure. If there is, it would be behind that wall they finished."

She contemplates this for a moment, then adds, "Hmmm... you know there's probably a corpse in there right?"

"Really, Bitch??!!!"

♀ ♂ ♀ ♂

It's go time again – date night. Dark denim skinny jeans, strappy heels, off-the-shoulder cream sweater, hair up and face flawlessly beat to the

Gawds ready to meet this entrepreneur, Silas, for our Not-Valentine's Day date. Just as expected, the entire town has beaten us to all of the usual celebratory locations, so we end up with an hour-long wait at T.G.I.Friday's. Of course, we met online because who can meet anyone out in public anymore? But he looks very much like his photos and has a sexy, confident swag for a short guy. These heels are putting me about four inches taller than him.

Can I date a man with more perfectly sculpted eyebrows than mine? I ponder this while we discuss his two children – a son and a daughter. I question if he gets to see them often considering divorce can be rough and bring about some hurt feelings. He casually tells me that he and his wife aren't divorced yet, they are merely separated.

"Oh, well when do you expect the divorce to be final?"

"We're not getting divorced until our son is at least fourteen. We want him to be a little older."

Ok, well he must be close to that, so I ask his age.

"He's seven."

There goes my face again. So this man is expecting me to date him while he stays married to his wife for the next *seven* years? Any clue as to what's *not* going to work for me? THIS SHIT! What, am I supposed to come over and snuggle up with him, his wife, and the kids and we all watch Netflix together on the couch? And when our relationship progresses to the next level, do we hang a sock on the front door? Or more than likely we're only ever having sex at *my* house for the next seven years. Or are we going to be sister wives? Oh, and *who* the hell is waiting seven more years to get married? Certainly not *me*! I have a biological clock situation ticking so loudly that it's keeping the cat up at night! I just have to know, "So, how is that whole thing working?"

"Well, we still live together for the kids but I sleep in the other room. Sometimes I sleep at my shop. I do my thing, she does hers, like roommates."

When he eventually excuses himself to go to the restroom, I hop onto my social media account and look up his wife. She is gorgeous. I can't even be a hater and call her a wombat. She isn't even close. According to him, she may have many faults, but she has flawless features, a well-sculpted body after two kids, and is educated and gainfully employed. Considering his body sculpture looks equally as delicious, there is nothing that can convince me that these two beautiful creatures aren't occasionally coming back together to bump uglies. While I understand that the depths of a marriage delve far deeper than anything merely aesthetic, basic chemistry, lust, comfort, and history all make for compelling lures to end up back in the other's bed.

Upon returning to the table, his phone begins to receive text messages back to back – messages that he is replying to promptly. He looks guilty but explains that it's still on in case there is an emergency with the kids. But he at least makes the wise decision to switch it to vibrate. He lays the phone back down face up and we continue our meal and conversation.

As the server is refilling our water, the entire table begins to vibrate and a giant photo pops up on the screen along with the words, "MY WIFE." Her lips close tightly together, her eyebrows raise and she looks at the two of us out on Valentine's Day weekend - while *his wife* is calling. AND HE'S ANSWERING THE CALL! Like, really!?

I am sitting across from this man watching our server walk away shaking her head, likely judging us both, while he chats with this woman on the phone. I guess I would expect to see the name change to her actual name, or "EX BOO" or something that would indicate that they are no longer together, but no. They are having a wonderfully friendly conversation. It's time to go.

As I gather my things, he hurriedly ends the call and requests that I stay and have dessert. His sweet smile and dimples make me stop to ponder it, but then his phone rings again and it's "MY WIFE."

"What for? You have been texting and talking to your wife all night. You should probably go be with her. Do you need some money for my burger or this tip?"

He declines my cash, which is a first, and asks that I at least stay until the bill is paid so he can walk me to my car. I'm not sure if he thinks he is getting a kiss or what, but these sexy, pouty beauties are staying put tonight. Showing off his gentlemanly side, he opens my car door and asks if he can see me again.

"Maybe," I say with a half-smile that really means absolutely not.

Add to my TO-DO list: Find Cupid and beat his little diapered ass

♀ ♂ ♀ ♂

As promised, I call Blaire to tell her about the outing. We're so not calling this a date because I don't "date" married men. Having this conversation through Bluetooth in my car, my raucous verbal outrage draws stares from neighboring vehicles at red lights, even with the windows up. But I don't care; I'm too old and tired for this drama! I can only envision the shock and awe on her face that I have seen so many times before when I've shared my dating disasters. I honestly think she pops popcorn when she sees my number on the caller ID because she knows it's about to be some foolishness. When she hears the last of my tale of woe, there is silence on the line, then in true Blaire fashion she blurts out, "I can't believe that fucker's married!"

She is so funny. So graceful and demure looking, but there's never any telling what might come out of her mouth. Sometimes it's delight and angels when she sings because she has a beautiful voice, then other times it's *that* special mess. It's part of her charm and appeal, I guess.

"So who else *is* there? Is that it? Oh no, Hassan is still around, right? You know, he never called for his massage."

Hassan *is* still around for the moment, though he absolutely shouldn't be. Just a few weeks back, he and I were watching football – on opposing sides. I had the Steelers and he had the losing team because as far as I'm concerned everyone else is garbage. I looked casual cute paying homage to my boo, Troy Polamalu, rockin' his #43 jersey with a pair of black leggings. He had on some revolting white jersey to cheer on his team of choice, who shall remain nameless.

I ordered a pizza, and during halftime, I mentioned that I should hit the walkway since it was snowing - lawsuits when pizza delivery drivers fall are not sexy. So I geared up in my winter apparel – coat, scarf, hat, gloves, boots – ready to shovel and salt for the safety of others. I just assumed that he would assist considering I am a woman shoveling heavy snow. But instead, from my sidewalk, I looked up to see this man waving to me from inside my cozy warm home while eating ALL of the red starbursts out of my candy jar!

I shoveled the front, so I figured I might as well do the side and back to maintain my good neighbor status and adhere to our town's snow ordinances. This was no small feat as my home, including the width of the driveway, literally spans 2/3 of that block. I also took the time to beat the snow off the car canopy that covers my beautiful, silver beauty. I then made multiple trips to salt the long sidewalk and driveway before coming in from the cold. My fingers were numb and the tip of my little chocolate nose was rouge by the time I once again sat beside him on the couch. He looked over at me and dared to ask, "What took you so long?"

Ever seen an exorcism? Well had I not been so damn cold, I might have looked like I needed one! Instantly, my body temperature increased because wow, had I had a *gentleman* helping me, it *wouldn't* have taken so long! This man stood there with not even the slightest thought or inclination to even bring me salt to expedite this snow removal process. While I understand that this is my home and ultimately the responsibility falls upon me to ensure the maintenance of my property, if the man who is trying to be in my life is that unwilling to lend a helping hand to get it done in half the time, what is his purpose? If he's going to make me be the man in the relationship as well, then I don't really need *his* ass.

Hassan went on to imply that it was my fault because I should've asked him to help me. I maintain that a real man doesn't need to be asked to help the woman he's trying to be with – especially with something as trivial as snow removal. And technically, I didn't *need* his help with that – I've been doing everything myself for so long that I've just grown accustomed to doing all the work alone. I figure, if a man wants to help, he will. It's that simple.

Add to my TO-DO list: Figure out which tree my soulmate is stuck in

CHAPTER 9
uninvited guests

I'm not sure how one single person, alone with a cat, can amass so much laundry. But until I can afford to pay someone else to do it for me, I'm stuck with it. In my apartment, the washer & dryer were right off the kitchen, but now they're in the basement. Yes, it's finished, but it's still a basement. Having lived in that two-bedroom apartment my entire life, all these extra levels are scary now – especially since these windows don't seem all that secure. I feel like anyone can just come in! *I gotta get some glass block down here ASAP*. I also always feel like I'm hearing weird noises and sounds. Voices. I googled the house to see if it was haunted or if there were any mysterious deaths on the property, but nothing surfaced. As I throw my light load into the washer, I still feel like I am hearing voices. Maybe Blaire is right. Maybe the cold cellar really *is* haunted by a corpse. The home*owner* in me wants to find out where they are coming from, but the home*girl* in me wants to burn the whole house down and start over. *Lemme get out of this creepy ass basement*!

As I ascend the cellar stairs, I am now positive I'm hearing voices. *Is someone in my HOUSE!? Oh HELL no*! I quietly return to the basement and find one of the large wooden planks that the previous owner left. Again, I ascend the stairs, turn the corner and run psychotically screaming into the living room with the wooden plank over my head, fully intending to scare whoever is there! Ariah is sitting on my couch scrolling through her phone, looking at me completely unfazed.

"What the hell is wrong with you?" she asks ever so casually.

"ME!?" Still frightened and breathing heavily, "What the hell is wrong with *you*!? How the hell did you get in my *house*!?"

"Bitch, I used my key."

"You don't *have* a key."

"Of *course* I have a key," She says like it's common knowledge.

I am so confused, but whatever, she's here now and has made herself comfortable so she's not leaving anytime soon. I slide my wooden plank down the basement steps and take a seat in the plush chair across the room from Ariah. As I begin to get comfy, I look over to see legs coming down my steps! How many people broke into my damn house since I went to throw towels in the washer? It's Brie coming from the upstairs bathroom smelling her hands.

"I love that soap! Hey girl!" Brie casually says like she was invited.

"Hi? How did you get *in* here?"

"What do you mean? Door was open."

"No, it *wasn't*!" I insisted resolutely.

"Yes it *was*, I have a *key*, bitch!" Ariah repeats like I am incapable of understanding this concept.

These two have made themselves at home in their footie socks because they know better than to walk through my house in shoes. They're both in hoodies and leggings like this was a coordinated attack. *Is this my intervention*? But turns out, they came separately and unbeknownst to the other.

"Is there anyone else in my house I need to know about?"

These harlots have the nerve to snicker and look at each other confused as to why I would ask such a ridiculous question when I wasn't even expecting *them* in my house. Once I'm content with the fact that there will be no more surprise arrivals in my home, I distribute hugs, grab the remote and turn on the music. My jam is playing so I immediately jump up and begin serenading my two college friends into the remote.

"On the ponntoooon... makin' waves and catchin' rays upon the rooooof..."

"No. NO. NOO!! Uh-uh! NOPE," they both yell in objection as I jam to Little Big Town's *Pontoon*. That's my stuff right there! I love some good country music!

"Party in slow motion... Out here in the open... mmmm motorboatinn," I sing while gyrating and inappropriately rubbing my body.

"What the *fuck* are we listening to!?" and other obscenities can be heard as I continue to evade them with the remote control. Finally, Ariah gets tired of fighting me for the remote and simply unplugs the surround sound. Curse her and her excess common sense.

"Where's this bitch's Black card? Go find her wallet! Over here listenin' to some damn country music! Consider that shit SUSPENDED," Brie says while dramatically going through my things.

"RIGHT!?" Ariah screams in agreement. "Look, we ordered some chicken once and got into her car to go get it and she had on some damn opera music, Brie. OPERA! I tried to hang tough but shit, I couldn't take it no more! Bitch, you know I tried to jump out of a moving car!?"

"Y'all are *so* dramatic! Country music is awesome! It really tells a story which you'd *know* if you'd just give it a shot! And it wasn't just *any* opera, it was the Jekyll and Hyde soundtrack! It's very dark and enjoyable! Damn!"

"*I* didn't enjoy it," Ariah says dramatically, shaking her head. "It wasn't enjoyable."

"Wow. Just wow. So why are y'all heifers here anyway? Don't like my music, don't like my potato salad... WHY. ARE. YOU. HERE?" I ask, laughing.

"Oooh yeah, that either," they both laugh.

"Uh-Uh, tasted like feet. You need to get your sister's recipe."

"FOCUS," I order as I snap my fingers.

Ariah hops up to pour herself a glass of wine. "Well, I met my girl for coffee across the bridge and figured I'd stop by. Hell, you're always home. I knocked but you didn't answer, so I used my key."

"Yeah, *about* that..."

"Pour me somma that too, please," Brie interrupts, shouting to Ariah like my house is *so* large. It's not. "I got rid of my kid *and* my husband, so I wanted to see quiet friends. Most of my girls have young kids or a man – you have neither and like Ri said, you're always here." Brie hands her engraved *Golden Girls* "Blanche" glass to Ariah intending to toast with me and my "Rose" glass. Ariah felt left out having left her "Dorothy" glass at home since her visit was more spontaneous.

"Thank you tramps for rubbing it in that I have no man, no kids, nowhere to go, and nothing to do.

Except maybe call a therapist now," I state with a heavy eye roll to accompany my exasperated tone.

Brie regards my sour expression with pursed lips. "Pour this uptight bitch some, too," she recommends to Ariah, super seriously.

"Nope I'm good. Still recovering from last night."

"Oooh, what happened last niiight?" Ariah asks as she serves Brie her drink.

"And was it good?" Brie asks in her sexy voice.

I can always count on Brie's nosey ass to inquire about the quality of said romantic interactions. She wants to know about it on a scale of 1-10, how many stars were involved, and if he stuck the dismount.

"I was with Sam last night and there really are no words to describe it."

"Awwwww shiit!! Okay!" Brie exclaims.

"Wait," Ariah says mid-sip. "Is he the super metrosexual one with all the shoes?"

"I mean, he's *something*."

Maybe he *is* just double *extra* metro. Either way, it all became too much for me. The first time visiting Sam's house, he was supposed to be ready at 6:00 p.m. When I arrived, he was still in his bath towel, water droplets covering his freshly showered, well-sculpted, mocha body. Usually, it's the women who are late when men arrive, not the other way around.

Clearly, we would need to talk about this punctuality thing. His apartment was eerily pristine – probably more so than mine and I'm a bit of a neat freak. Everything had a place but there was *no* place for dust. The entire room had a very disinfected yet warm feel with tastefully artsy décor and amply plumped throw pillows to match. Even the color coordination seemed to be on point and flowed from room to room. I was actually excited to be in a man's house who could keep one as well as I could. Let's be real – probably better than I could.

He shouted out to me that he was mostly dressed if I wanted to come back to the bedroom, so I did and took a seat at the foot of his bed. Inside Sam's walk-in closet was a most disturbing sight. Shoes. Everywhere – dress shoes, tennis shoes, golf shoes, casual shoes, water shoes, sandals, you name it. I would wager that there were easily four times the amount of shoes any normal woman would own from what I could tell from my position on the bed.

Still chatting while he was getting ready, he went into the bathroom to put in his contacts. I took it upon myself to glance into this wasteland of apparel to see for myself if maybe my eyes were deceiving me. Sadly, they were not and it was even worse than I thought. These shoes lined up rows deep. All of the clothing was hung as if freshly out of the cleaners – all Calvin Klein. The button-downs, tees, pants, undershirts, hats, belts, socks, and boxers. ALL Calvin. Even some of the shoes. I was beginning to wonder if I would find a CK branded on this dude's ass. Hanging up were more ties than I owned socks and there were even more belts than ties. I thought, Eh, I guess this is normal for a professional man until he later told me about his blue-collar job that he doesn't even wear a shirt and tie to perform.

I had no idea what he was doing in that bathroom but *why* was it taking so long? I'm a girl and it's never taken me that long to get ready. So I strolled over to the dresser where I found more watches than I owned earrings. WHY? Sports watches, smart watches, casual watches, leather watches in all shades, scuba watches – like damn! How much time do you need to *tell*!? I have a watch. As in one - it's two-tone so it goes with my darks and my neutrals. Then there really *was* a spot that housed more earrings than I own, along with every size carat of diamond from which to select – and again, he can't wear *any* of them to work. Along the entire width of the dresser were rows and columns of colognes – many of them Calvin Klein, of course. I consider myself to be a bit of a fragrance whore, owning the bulk of the Victoria's Secret Garden collection among many other finer scents, but this man is putting me and all of the women I know to shame.

The next twelve minutes were spent at the dresser while Sam tried to figure out the appropriate watch/earring/fragrance combo to compliment his *whole* Calvin Klein outfit. Then onto the correct shade of Calvin socks and matching Calvin shoes. Almost an hour later he was finally ready to go.

"He probably looked *and* smelled better than you," Ariah laughs.

"GIRL! You *know* he did! Hell by the time he got ready, my make-up was all worn off, my curls had fallen and I was lookin' a hot busted-ass mess."

"Wow, yeah that's a lot. I don't know about a man who spends more time on his actual appearance than I do. That's ummm..."

"Brie," I interrupt. "I'm talkin' facials, mani/pedis, lip treatments, all that. I don't know... it's sexy when my overly manly man with busted feet wants to get a pedicure so his wildebeest hooves don't tear up my sheets. But when you *already* have prettier feet than me and schedule bi-weekly maintenance pedicures? That's just a little *much*... like, I don't know what to think!"

"Oh see, you ain't tell me all *that*!" Ariah interjects. "He's doin' *way* too much."

"RIGHT? And he has such a soft voice! Like I wake up in the morning with more bass in my shit than he has by dinner time! But he was cool and we had fun so I'm seeing him again tomorrow afternoon to further assess. I'll keep y'all tricks posted."

"I think he'll do better this time," Ariah predicts confidently.

Brie and I both look at her like she belongs in a white jacket that helps her hug herself.

"Gimme this," Brie takes Ariah's glass. "Clearly, you been drinkin' too much. Time to sober up, Dorothy!"

Add to TO-DO list: Change the fucking locks – ALL of them

♂ ♀ ♂ ♀

Ariah is wrong. *So* incredibly wrong. I need to snap a picture of this. Jumping out of a clean, gold Toyota Sequoia, because he's too damn short to simply step out of the oversized SUV, is a man dressed like he's about to captain the S.S. Minnow. Naturally, the entire ensemble is Calvin Klein - a navy blue collar tee with matching navy slacks, a ribbed white sweater vest with matching white socks, and shoes. The partial tuck of the vest displays the navy/silver belt that matches the watch and sunglasses. And atop his bald head is a white Calvin Klein bucket hat like the ones women put on their infants at the beach to protect their little faces from the UV rays. This might be fine if we were on a yachting expedition, except we are at the indoor mall for a simple shopping trip and a casual lunch.

He waves excitedly to me and I'm hoping I've managed to arrange a polite smile while waving back in confusion because I'm really not sure what to make of it all. He smells great though when he hugs me; of course with the 249.4 fragrances he owns, he damn well better. We begin to walk through the mall and window shop until we find a store we're interested in perusing.

"You want some gum? It's sugar-free."

Oh gosh is my breath hot like all those dudes?

"Sure. Thanks."

When he offers me the pack, I notice it's not mint-flavored gum to cover mouth funk, it's bubble gum flavor which means it's pink. *This grown-ass man chews PINK gum. I don't even chew pink gum!* I take a piece and begin to open it.

"You have to take two."

"I'm fine with one, thanks though."

"Well I chew it in increments of two, so if you could just take two, that'd be helpful."

Y'all *know* I'm looking at him like he's a whole sociopath as I wordlessly take an additional piece of gum and drop it into my purse for future chewing.

He pops two pieces into his mouth because Heaven forbid he chew just one like normal people.

Bath & Body is having their $3 sale on hand soaps, so we venture in. I quickly find numerous soaps in my favorite scents to not bore this man in the girly shop. But when I look over, I notice he has an entire shopping basket full of soaps as well.

"Mmm... This sweet pea one is *really* nice," Sam murmurs, inhaling appreciatively.

"Oh. Uh... Yeah it is. I have that one too. Are you getting it as a gift for someone?"

"Oh noo, this is for ME! And this Lemoncello will go great in my kitchen. Think I should buy some of these decorative covers for them?"

"Umm... I have them on all three of mine. So maybe?" I share with him one of the more virile scents I'm purchasing. "What do you think about this teakwood?"

"Nah, that's a little dark smelling. I'm cool with these."

"Ooookay."

So we both checkout and I am now walking through the mall with a man dressed like a sailor carrying a bag from Bath & Body that clearly isn't mine since I have one too. Ok.

The same thing happens in the candle store – I gravitate to all the heavier, stereotypically masculine fragrances and he leaves with scents that would make one assume that the sales clerk switched our bags. We then wander into Victoria's Secret and I think for *sure* there is nothing in here that this man can leave with but apparently, I am as mistaken as Ariah was. As I'm selecting panties to buy with this coupon, I spy Sam in the fragrance section. I know this man likes scents but *damn*. I'm watching with raised eyebrows as he sprays them on the paper sample stick like a seasoned pro and airs them out before taking a whiff. I guess he decides upon Love Spell. At least he has good taste. He approaches me in the checkout line and I look at the body spray and then up at him.

"Soooo..." Not really knowing what question to ask here.

"Oh, I like to add this to my Febreze!"

I can feel my eyes narrow slightly, observing him to assess if he's being truthful or if he's just shopping for some other chick while we're together. But he *seems* dead ass serious. I mean his house *did* smell super extra fresh when I visited.

"You should try it – gives it so much more punch!"

Yeah. So we both checkout and I am now walking through the mall with a man dressed like a sailor carrying bags from Bath & Body, Yankee Candle, and Victoria's Secret, which again clearly aren't mine since I have them too. Oo-kayyy.

The shopping excursion continues and gets more awkward with each store because what does an adult male need from Claire's? I'm hearing something about his earring backs, but it's hard to focus when a grown-ass man is smacking on pink gum. I decide to run into Perfumania across the hall while Sam handles his man business in Claire's. He joins me when he's finished and makes a purchase here as well. Never mind the fact that he could scent the entire state of Texas with the amount of fragrance on his dresser.

Yup. So again, we both checkout and - you guessed it. I am now walking through the mall with a man dressed like a sailor carrying bags from Bath & Body, Yankee Candle, Victoria's Secret, Claire's, and Perfumania. And to top it off, he is now *blowing pink bubbles* like he's the shit walkin' through this mall! *None* of this is *okay* for me!

I'm not feeling the food court right now and kind of have a taste for some fast food, which pretty much never happens. So we agree upon one and place our orders. I go through the bag to make sure it's correct and then we pull out and find a spot to park and eat. When we're done, I ask a question - the most normal question in the world. Something I assume every car owner does because I've never been in a car after a drive-thru and *not* seen it happen. Here goes.

"Do you want me to put these napkins in your glove box?" I remove about six from the empty bag and make them neat and presentable.

"Nah baby, I got puffs."

"Excuse me?"

Because I heard it but I feel like I need to hear it again to verify that I heard what I thought I heard. You hear me?

"I got PUFFS!" Sam whips open his glove box and, sure enough, there was a full box of ultra-soft Puffs Kleenex ready for use. I feel like as much as he cleans, he should know that some damn Puffs aren't going to work effectively if there's a spill, but whatever. He can use his Puffs and I will take these napkins to MY car where we have good sense.

Sam drops me back off where I'm parked at the mall and we hug goodbye. He really is a sweet guy, but I'm just not sure about some of these tendencies. It's just very different for me. I also find myself needing to know how common this pink gum thing is among men, though. So I immediately text my best guy friend, Tyce.

Renee: Hey. Question. What kind of gum do you chew?

Tyce: Winter fresh. Why?

Renee: You chew bubble gum at all?

Tyce: HELL naw!! WHY?

Renee: Do your boys chew pink bubble gum?

Tyce: Da FUQ!?

I'll take that as a no. And of course, now my phone is ringing and I get to explain the reason for the queries. He lets me know he'll be by this weekend for a drink and a smoke.

Add to my TO-DO list: Buy stock in Calvin Klein so I can at least benefit from the emotional shopping Sam does when I end it

CHAPTER 10
porch playtime, part 1

It's a beautiful, breezy spring day, and as promised, Tyce pops up for a porch visit with his infamous blue beverage that inevitably leaves me hungover regardless of how little I drink. But it tastes like a blue Icee so who can turn *that* down? I always look forward to the random drive-by visits when we can catch up on work, life, and just cut up and chill. This tall, dark chocolate, clean-cut man walks into the house like he paid the mortgage this month and makes the drinks. He knows I'm a lightweight and makes mine with three-parts Sprite, one-part blue juice which turns it the color of Windex. I light my cigar along with the fire table on the porch to warm up the outdoor area.

Tyce, with his large, football player frame, gets comfy because, like many of my colleagues and girlfriends, he too enjoys hearing all the crazy that happens with my disaster dates. So I quickly tell him about, Norris, the man who told me that I don't make a man "feel like a man" because I had assembled all the items in my home and installed my own flooring. Let him tell it, that's man's work. To make matters worse, after eating me out of house and home, he *then* threw away his paper plate *and* my expensive ass dinner fork! This man paused at the garbage can for a few seconds contemplating whether or not he should go in to retrieve it but decided against it. He didn't know that I saw him do it until I yelled, "Now go get it!" But I digress, according to him, I'm supposed to call a man, invite him over and cook him a nice, hearty meal, then ask *him* to fix or assemble anything I need to be handled in my home.

Tyce giggles in shock, "Look grasshoppa, I feel like I've trained you well enough to know that a man does *not* want to assemble your grill after eating a good meal. He don't wanna assemble *shit*! Not repair shit, not *do* shit! He wants..."

"Good head or to go to sleep, " I proclaim like I have the winning answer on Jeopardy.

"And let us all raise our glasses in a toast," he laughs. So we do.

"That guy woulda shit a *bird* if I'd have told him about when Ariah bought her house and I went over with my fully stocked, masculine toolbox and did so many *manly* repairs to it that by the time I left, I was her boyfriend! She might not have known it, but I was her boo!"

Tyce has spent the last twenty years of our friendship telling me what "normal" men want and all the seemingly common sense things that the women in his life have or haven't done that he and other men find annoying or frustrating. He also shares all the TMI things men don't usually want to hear that women usually *don't* think are TMI. I can always call him when men are doing something stupid so I can gain insight into their thought processes, though he isn't able to help much with poor Troy.

We're chilling on the porch watching cars cruise through the stop sign on my fairly heavily traveled street and I tell him about the recent ax-throwing date I had with Troy. I should've known something was wrong with him when he told me that he drove a Toyota CR-V.

"Hold up, that's not even a thing," Tyce laughed.

I just test-drove every SUV ever made, I know this, but after calling him out on that information, he decided that he drove a Toyota Rav-4. He talked hella smack on the phone all the way to the ax-throwing venue, where they also offer bowling and other arcade games.

"Wait, ya'll really went *ax-throwin'*!?"

I then have to listen to Tyce laugh and clown me about how he *knows* we were the only Black folks there – he ain't lyin' though. Country music, white people, and us. But most of my friends are white anyway, so I was right at home - Gimme an ax!

So even though he was late, Troy arrived *still* talking crap about how he was gonna lay the smack down on me, but it's fine because I have a slick mouth as well. I talked that smack right back! Another couple was paired up to compete with us, which I thought would be fun. So now that meant we no longer had to compete against each other, we just had to team up to smash *them*, right? Wrong.

When I carried us through the first game scoring the majority of the points, I got *no* acknowledgment. No high fives, no "good job," nothing. Like, dude, we are the only Black people in here and we are *winning*! With *axes*! He wouldn't even make eye contact with me. When he was carrying us through the second game and I threw up my hands to high five, he would walk right past me, still with no reaction. The couple on the other team began to root for me and take photos of me with my phone to commemorate the event since Troy wasn't wanting to be involved. I began to feel like I should call them again for a second date since it went better with them than it did with him.

I thought *surely* he would want to end the date after that because he clearly didn't seem interested after being beaten by a girl at a "man's sport" as he called it, but he elected to stay and suggested we play arcade games. I humbly warned him that I was a skillful competitor and that I didn't keep a power card in my wallet for shits and giggles. When a woman pulls out a game card, that means she has been getting practice whoopin' on simple, naïve fools like *you* who underestimate her. That means "play these games with her at your own egotistical risk."

With a shoulder injury, I beat him by just under twenty points in basketball, at which point he claimed that the score counter was broken. So we played again and when he won, I asked if the score was correct that time. Naturally, he said it was. So when we broke the tie and I won, it was mysteriously broken again. This man's ego was so fragile that he couldn't handle losing to a woman in an arcade basketball game. Even though he would have had me for breakfast in a real game because I'm no good under actual pressure.

Moving on to Skeeball, I figured I would let him win because he didn't know that I am the reigning International Skeeball Champ – ok, not really, but I feel like it the way I hit those top corner 10,000's with regularity. Upon his false victory, he began to loudly gloat and proclaim how he dominated me and I just stood there like, *really dude? I gave you that win, so now I have to take these two out of three to show you who I am because you're being a DICK.* So I easily and silently won the next two games and mysteriously, the score counter was wrong again and I somehow miraculously had more balls than he did. That was the only reason I won, according to him.

He then decided that he wanted to bowl and I thought to myself, *there is no WAY I'm subjecting myself to that torturous hell.* If I beat that man bowling, he would lose his entire religion and I didn't sign up for that crazy. Besides, he only made eye contact with me long enough to revel in false victory and that was really the only time he spoke to me the entire evening. He clearly wasn't interested in me romantically, and that was fine. Though he was a very attractive man physically, his egotistical behavior was a huge turn-off.

My shiny new car was already running, warming up under the glow of the overhead streetlight when we approached. Even though I was ready to get away from this man, I asked if he needed a ride to his car but he pointed across the lot, indicating that he was parked nearby. I casually mentioned that his SUV is not a Toyota, but a brand new Mercedes Benz, and I asked why he lied about his vehicle. This man stood in front of me and pursed his deceitful lips to say, "I didn't lie." *WTF!? You're lying right NOW about lying!* Unless Mercedes makes a RAV-4, yes he did lie. He alluded to the fact that he didn't want a woman who only wanted him for his possessions.

"Yo, where you be findin' these dudes, man!?" Tyce interjects. "Did this fool not see that you have a brand new car your damn self? Does he know your shit still smells like the factory? Your shit still got the plastic stuff on the floors!"

"Right!? I'm not checkin' for his car! That's insulting! My baby girl is top of the line! We have the same amenities; I was just smart enough to pay $23,000 less. What I *am* checkin' for is someone who isn't gonna *lie* to me about it!"

Tyce raises his index finger to the sky, "And let the church say..."

"AMEN," we laugh. "But wait, it gets worse. Then he sent this text when I got home... Not checking to see if I got home ok or anything though... Lemme find it..."

I hand my phone to Tyce to read the message himself so he can see that I am by no means making this up or exaggerating.

Troy: I guess you didn't like me enough to let me tie you up and have my way with you.

"WHOOOAAHH!!" Tyce almost drops the phone! "Was he serious!?"

"Absolutely."

"Ok well, they can't *all* be crazy online. There have to be *some* normal ones on there somewhere. Right?" Wrong.

Well not *totally* wrong. I have met my share of seemingly normal men online, but sometimes two people meet and just aren't on the same page. In some of these situations, we weren't even in the same book. Like my ex who knew I didn't have children and that I wanted at least one but he already had a vasectomy and outright lied to me about it for *years*. Did he think that I wouldn't find out eventually? This isn't rocket science – sperm meets egg and when it doesn't, the doctor comes in and tells you which one of you needs some repair work. In this situation, he didn't need fixed; he had already *been* fixed and hidden it. He claimed that he didn't believe I would have dated him had I known. Maybe he is right, but wasting years of my functional fertility with lies was not the way to keep us solid.

Others I have met seemed ok but had work schedules that drastically conflicted with mine, thus they had no time to invest in another person or were simply happy remaining unmarried and just dating forever. A few who hadn't yet been sterilized simply didn't want any more children and I still do. Like I said, just not on the same page.

"And for the ones who aren't even in the same *library*? I have an entire folder of screenshot messages on my phone. I'mma pull 'em up, hold on."

I locate the folder and hand Tyce the phone so that he can scroll through it and see the crazy firsthand. "You wouldn't believe some of the senseless things these men say online."

Return Of The Mack: I won't tolerate women with tattoos and Black women with ink just show how low class, trashy & ignorant they are.

"Oh! Don't you have like five?" Tyce inquires.

"Eight. Granted, they're all in discreet locations so my man has to play hide-and-seek to find 'em. But once he started sayin' how he also wouldn't tolerate white women, large women, and other peoples' children, it was time to end that conversation, so I hung up. I don't fall into any of those latter categories, but I still found the whole conversation disgusting. Everyone is entitled to their preferences, but *tolerate* though?"

Tyce shakes his head and gets back to scrolling through the mess – I mean mess*ages*.

Me: So what do you do for a living?

Nate Dogg: I'm just coming home from doing 7 years in the feds for firearm possession.

Tyce looks over at me with a raised brow as if to inquire why every man straight out the joint wants to date me.

"Oh no, there was another one who told me that he had a few lawsuits he was working on so I'm over here thinkin' I found a legitimate lawman. Turns out, what he meant was, he was *actually* in the middle of a few lawsuits so we couldn't do anything active for a date because he was being watched. And once these were over, he would file new lawsuits elsewhere. So he's just out here makin' a living via fraud! He's about to be watched in the state pen and he can do all that without me."

Tyce is still staring at me like I'm crazy before scrolling through to the next messages.

Mr. Elite 77: Hey baby can I wash your hair and massage your feet?

Mr. Elite 77: You there?

Mr. Elite 77: Whatever.

Mr. Elite 77: So I can't bite that booty?

Looking4Her: I want to financially support you. If you're not fully attracted to me I will consider an open marriage to give you the flexibility you want. But I will still be monogamous to you.

GQSmoove: RITE NOW IM IN PRISON FOR A MINOR FEDERAL VIOLATION A FEW MONTHS AT THE MOST 9TO EXACT. I HOPE YOU CAN TAKE A POSSITIVE CHANCE IN GET TO NOW ME

BeaverEater: We should get married lol wanna eat your pussy so bad give you a massage

BeaverEater: I been wanting you - always thought you lived so far away

BeaverEater: Love Libras OMG

BeaverEater: Want your ass and pussy in my face so bad

"Clearly he missed the 'snack box' memo. And why is everyone trying to massage you?" Tyce asks, laughing.

"RIGHT!? No clue, but you see I didn't respond. And yes, he got blocked."

BigPen1: Men in your area can't handle your independents. But I can… There's a twist. I'm in jail finishing a sentence in the feds since 2007. I come home in 10 months so we can use this time to build.

Tyce smirks and jokingly bats his lashes and asks, "What ch'all 'bout to build togevvaa?" He's always cuttin' up and acting simple.

Me: How was your holiday?

SouthernGent2: Absolutely fabulous because my family is going through a very traumatic situation with my sister murdering our mother so it was nothing but whole lot of love in our house. Can I call you?

"Yooo! Keep these people away from your mother!" Tyce laughs.

IHeartFeet69: Damn your kitchen clean in that pic. You must got pretty feet. I just want to put my mouth on them toes. Would you paint them red like little cherries for me?

AssMan1: Your jugs are amazing!!!!!!!

"I mean this last guy wasn't lyin' though," Tyce says with a smirk and a shrug. "Even though he's an AssMan."

Laughing, "I *know* this, but it's not how I care to be approached by a man. Especially when the bulk of said jugs aren't even out to play in the photos! And these aren't even *all* of them! These are just the ones I have saved. These men have no class or clue as to how to talk to a woman."

While that idiot's over there not *tolerating* white women, I don't tolerate disrespect. These men are not going to come at me all crazy and think it's acceptable – it's not. One guy got all flustered when telling me that women don't listen to him. About what? Anything. He said they act like they want to obey, then they get a title and start acting all bossy. He said he needs to put his foot down and be respected as a man. Well, what the hell is going on in his relationships that he needs to do all that to get respect as a man?

"Wait," I exclaim. "You need to see *this* psychotic ass profile." I open up the dating app and find the man who viewed my profile. Neither of us is sure what's happening in *any* of his photos he has posted. There are guns, middle fingers, weed, gold teeth, and *way* too much random cash lying around. *Most* legitimate jobs end with a direct deposit somewhere. His just looks like it's being stored in a shoebox under the bed.

I handed the phone back to Tyce so he could read the extremely eloquently written profile.

My name Dre. I stay in EAs Liberty and I have 4 kids. THEY HALF WHITE AND I ONLY DATE A WHITE GURL. So, if you aint WHite, leave me alone! They mama take drug and I gots full cusody. I like to hump it and bump it and pump it and kick it! You know jus hanging out and see what happens. Lets see wat happens. I do candle lit dinners with fancy foo. I am TALL and athletic and got it going on! I like to keep it real. My kids is MIX half white and half black

YOU must have your own car cuz I dont gots one. I AM A TALL Black man so I like to get down! i only date white with no our eyes. All you UGLY women with the four eyes take you nasty face elsewhere.

I AM A BORN AGAIN BELIEVER IN CHRIST JESUS AND LONG TO SERVE HIM

"Wowww, my head hurts! That took *way* longer than it should've to be able to read and comprehend! And what the hell is fancy foo?" Tyce asks, laughing in disbelief. "Man, I'm glad I'm married and not dealing with *this* kind of dumbness. I don't know how you *do* it. On a brighter note – hopefully, how's the new neighbor?"

"Anyone not waking me up with obnoxious sex wailing and booming headboard banging is *great* in my book!"

The new neighbor, Gabriel, is terrific so far. Ironically, he's also from Puerto Rico but has no accent. Good thing my Spanish is coming along well. After my last experience, I was praying for a functional person to move in, so when a bald, older, gay, Hispanic man knocked on my door and introduced himself, I was like yasss hunny! Love it! I have a large handful of gay and lesbian friends and I say love who you want to love because it doesn't change what I'm doing right now or how many dishes are in my sink.

Gabriel has a psychotic little Lhasa Apso named Sadie, who thinks she's a Great Dane. She needs prayer and a shock collar. Sadie barks incessantly and doesn't like *anyone* but I gave her cheese once and now we're best friends. She whines until I pet her and nuzzle my head to hers. Even though Gabriel and Sadie live alone, in true Puerto Rican fashion, there is always a large gathering of family visiting. Even when there isn't, he cooks as though there is, which means there is always a ton of extra arroz con habichuelas and whatever other flavorful cuisine he's preparing! If he keeps feeding me all this amazing food, I'm going to have to butter down the door to get my thick ass through it.

"Well, that's what's up, cuz I already know that you only cook so you don't die."

"Ooooh, facts! How's *your* new job?" I ask.

"I love it! I'm so much happier there," Tyce replies contentedly. "A little more diversity would be nice though, but I know you can relate."

"Absolutely, I'm the only person of any color at my new position as well. It definitely is exhausting and would be nice to interact with anyone who could understand how I feel on any given day."

"Ditto," Tyce agrees, "But I don't see that happening anytime soon."

♂ ♀ ♂ ♀

Once my old friend has gotten me sufficiently tipsy, he goes on his way and I go back in the house to try to recover. OMG, it's like an epidemic up in *here*! I check the caller ID – random dude who stood me up at the burger joint *three months* ago called to finally apologize and ask for a re-do. *No.* Dude who packed up my food because he was on parole got a new phone number and is *still* calling. *No.* Talkative dude who just won't *stop* ringing my phone, he called – four times – in a row. *Why can't the man of my dreams just call!?* Last week, that same talkative guy called three times, then I woke up the next morning to find two online messages - one of which simply read, "I called you." He also left two video calls and a video message that said, "Hello?" Dude, go get a drink because you are #thirsty. This is why I refuse to hand out my cell number. If he's doing all this *before* sex (which will never happen), I can't even imagine what would happen *after*! He'd probably try to move in.

Add to my TO-DO list: Change my home phone number

CHAPTER 11
the thing

Somehow my life has always followed the creepy trend of being laid off roughly three months after any large-scale purchase. After the lease of my Chevy, the purchase of my home, and the next lease of my Hyundai, I was either laid off or contracts ended on all three of those positions. I need to stop buying shit, for real!

The interview process has been a grueling one but fortunately, securing a new position in my field happened relatively quickly. I anticipated it taking much longer after my last interview when I was asked, "Please give me a three-minute synopsis of your entire life." *Really lady? The whole thing? Three minutes?*

"What kind of crystal meth do you use?" *What the SHIT!? Are these really on that paper?*

"How many times in the past month have you physically fought a co-worker?" *WOWW! NONE, lady! Is this some secret cage-fighting position or WHAT!??*

I *know* my facial expressions were all over the place in that interview. I was later saved by a more standard group of interviewers who offered me the position without inquiring about my hardcore SmackDown skills. I figure I will have this job for roughly 2.6 years before I have to renew my lease and then, because Karma still hates me, this trend will continue, resulting in my inevitable layoff.

Dani arrives late to the office, her brunette curls all disheveled, and slams her purse onto the desk. Visibly and audibly annoyed, she approaches my cube and rambles a tale of disgust – I'm not catching it all because she hasn't had her coffee yet. But it's something about a chipmunk, some dirt, a giant rock, her pool, and a fake frog. *Bitch, go get some coffee already*. When she returns, she alludes to the fact that she's heard through the grapevine that I have some outlandish stories about my crazy dating life. *Oh gosh, is this about to happen again?*

So you know how there's always that one co-worker who thinks she should be in charge? That one colleague who behaves like she's the boss of everything? Well, this definitely *isn't* Dani, but it absolutely *could* be. With the most knowledge and insight out of everyone in the office, she offers an organized chaos that oddly, everyone seems to respect. Much like my sister, Dani is not able to get anywhere on time either, like ever. But she makes us all laugh, so her presence makes an otherwise cramped workplace bearable. We have developed a rather dysfunctional relationship such that if anyone dares to make mention of how damaged we are as a pair, we break out into an off-key melody of Danity Kane's song *Damaged* to further prove our instability, or so maybe they will eventually leave us the hell alone.

If I'm the Queen of the Germophobes, that makes Dani the Princess. It's only been a few weeks but we already have an understanding and have developed our own set of social cues to know when to disinfect the other. Then one of us, in dramatic flair, will break out the Lysol hand sanitizing spray and Spritz the other down while singing and gyrating to the Li'l Boosie song *Wipe Me Down*. While it is wonderful to be in the office with someone who is as weirdly germophobic as I am, it must be said that somehow I was the only one taken to human resources and asked by the HR Director why I wash my hands and sanitize my workstation daily.

What an odd question. Some better questions are "Why is my cleanliness weird to you?" and "Why don't you wash YOUR hands?" Maybe it was because I also asked for the hermetically-sealed bubble from the movie *E.T.* around my cube? But I feel like common sense would dictate that I was joking. *Clearly not.* And now the running joke in the office when anyone says anything inappropriate is, "Oh my gosh, we're all going to end up in HR." Then someone will inevitably say, "Well not *all* of us," implying that only I will have to go, which makes us all laugh. I can make light of it with them solely because I don't believe that these particular colleagues have any actual malicious intent. They, along with all of my other friends and family, were just as appalled to hear about it as I was to live through that ridiculous and superfluous HR event.

"Tell me one of your stories before I have to bury myself in work. It'll take my mind off that stupid chipmunk," Dani requests enthusiastically.

Ugh yes, it IS happening again, but I'm more interested in hearing about that chipmunk. Another equally fascinated colleague hears her request and quickly comes forward as well in hopes that I will comply since she must've been in the grapevine with Dani's ass. I now have two ladies, both grandmothers, leaning over the edge of my cube in suspense, so I must be selective about which story I choose to tell them. Nothing too racy - wouldn't want to end up in HR – again. Unlike the guy I spoke to the other night who told me that two men turned him in for sexual harassment. Well, my first question was, what did you say to two grown-ass men that made them feel harassed enough to take it to management? He claimed he didn't know what he said and that he talks about women a lot so that was probably it. No part of that story sounded right so I had to end that conversation.

I figured they could appreciate the date I had with Larry more than I could. He and I were planning to meet in an area of town that is a bit more upscale. I am a huge proponent of dressing for one's location, so I wanted to let him know this. That way he could dress accordingly and not show up in sweats like previous daters. He told me that he was planning to wear just jeans and a tank top. Let's be honest here, I don't know too many Black men who own legitimate tank tops, so I felt compelled to clarify if this was in fact a tank top or a wife beater, which I really wouldn't deem appropriate for this location. We're already under constant scrutiny and judgment, let's not worsen it with our attire today, please. He admits that it's a wife-beater. *Sigh.* Some bodies should never just come out of the house in an undershirt, others like Diego's can pull it off with ease. So in an effort to gauge whether or not this man had a "with ease" situation, I had to ask, "You must have a nice body if you can pull off wearing *just* a beater?" He confirmed that he was in construction so his body was right.

As I waited seated on the bench outside the ice cream shop scrolling through social media on my phone, I saw a figure in the distance that could've possibly been him. I was wearing my contacts but since I have an astigmatism, my far sight isn't as clear as it should be. That's what I get for being vain and not wearing my glasses. The closer the figure came, the more I realized that people are really not self-aware at *all*! Larry's portly midsection was stuffed into this greyish-yellowish wife beater that was probably white when it was first taken out of the package. Looking like he was about to give birth any minute, his stomach hung over a pair of black jeans with a brown belt. As he drew even closer, there was a noticeable yellow stain around the left nipple area. I wasn't sure if he was lactating because he was about to drop that baby or what, but it was cool because we were just down the street from the hospital – and I did not need Maury to tell me that I was *not* the mother!

Larry smiled at me with teeth the color of his shirt and went in for a hug despite my hesitation. While his man boobs were pressed against my woman boobs, I could feel an abundance of hair coming from his armpits that grew down his arms, up his shoulders, and connected around his neck. It basically looked like someone put a wife beater on a bear. As I stood there wondering how he felt this look was appropriate attire for a first date, I was no longer interested in a stroll through this upscale community with my frozen delight.

We entered the fro-yo shop where I found the smallest infant-sized cup available, squirted the tiniest schmutz of yogurt imaginable, and added one light dusting of topping. The plan was to swallow that in one gulp and get the hell out of there. He asked if I wanted to take a walk since he purchased a much larger treat, but I politely declined that offer. I was in *no* mood for witnessing him being erroneously hunted because he was mistaken for Sasquatch.

My colleagues are bent over each other laughing, probably more so at my tone, facial expressions, and the *way* I verbally tell a story than the actual story itself. As the ladies return to their cubes still laughing, I hear, "That was so great! She needs her own podcast or something!"

Add to my TO-DO list: Get this damn astigmatism fixed

♂ ♀ ♂ ♀

Standing in front of a totally packed freezer and refrigerator with the French doors wide open, I think about how my Nana would be chastising me for letting all the cold air escape. There is so much food in here but it all needs to be cooked and who the hell wants to do *that* after the terribly stressful day I've had?

DING DING

Jackson: Hey. Wanna come over for dinner? I'm cooking.

What timing! But HELL no. Hard pass. Nope. Uh uh. Delete.

DING DING

Jackson: It'll be something you like!

Not likely. Of course, a very handsome Jackson and I met online and we went for an ice cream date, right? Wrong. Because Jackson doesn't eat actual *food*! No dairy, no lactose, no gluten, no sugar, no carbs, no meat, no fun!! What's left? The most disturbing part is that he doesn't not eat them because he has health issues or allergies to them, he just doesn't *want* to. This psychotic yet fundamental difference in lifestyle is among the many reasons that he and I are just friends. The reality is this man needs a quarter-pounder with cheese, STAT! I could never understand it when I would hear men say they didn't want to date a skinny woman but preferred a woman with a little thickness. I get it now. This dating experience has enlightened me that being *that* much thicker than my man brings out some of my own bodily insecurities and just doesn't make me feel sexy. Therefore, I can only imagine arriving at this man's apartment to eat some veggie tofu dish when all I really want is some meat and carbs with sugar for dessert, please.

Renee: Thank you so much for the offer, but I already have something on the stove 😊

Siiigh, now what the hell am I gonna put on this stove?

The phone dings yet again as my annoyance grows. No means no, man! But it's just Sam asking if he can swing by on his way home from some event later this evening. Why not? I literally have nothing else planned and he's the only person who I've seen more than once in the past probably eight months. I'm not feeling any sexy vibes or romantic chemistry between us – on *my* end anyway. They say it's in the kiss – yeah, it wasn't there. I looked twice. It kind of felt like I was kissing my sister because his lips were almost too soft from all his facial treatments, his lashes were longer than mine and he smelled... pretty all the time. I kind of just need my man to smell like one – a ruggedly good smelling one though.

When Sam finally makes it to my house to hang out, I have already eaten. Real protein, legit carbs, actual veggies, and genuine sugar for dessert - all the things that Jackson would've withheld from me. I am freshly showered with my long, pressed hair up in my go-to messy bun. Since I'm not going anywhere and it's just Sam, I'm comfy on the couch watching my DVR recording of the Serena Williams documentary in my favorite loungewear – a men's button-down top and a pair of Old Navy women's boxers. I get so excited re-watching portions of matches like I don't already know the outcome. I still get just as hype as if it's my first viewing.

I would expect one of Sam's array of fragrances, but it's the smell of spirits that hits me before Sam's body does when he gives me a giant bear hug! Though his level of intoxication is unclear as of yet, he has been drinking.

"Wowww... You look so sexy in that shirt. I should bring you one of mine to wear."

Oh yeah, he must be *super* drunk because he should damn well know that these mammoth breasts are not fitting into any of the tiny shirts he owns. Like dude, I am bigger than you are. He's eyeing me up like I'm a two-piece with a biscuit while removing and hanging up his sport coat. Because he probably needs to sober up a tad more before the remainder of his trip home, I run to the fridge to grab him a bottled water only to find that he has followed me into the kitchen.

Sam opens and takes a swig of the water, then runs his cold hand up my bare thigh and attempts to passionately kiss me. Except I am feeling zero desire, so I back out of it but he doesn't take the hint and continues to kiss down my neck to visit the twin peaks. Because he knows very little about me sexually, he is unaware that the *least* erogenous zone of my body is my breasts. Even Diego can barely turn me on playing on that playground and he's a master oral manipulator. But part of me is simply curious to see what's about to happen with this partially intoxicated man who doesn't seem to understand that BIG booby bras have at least *five* hooks. One drunken hand trying to remove body armor this size will never suffice.

It takes him a little longer than it should to get frustrated with trying to be smooth and he just lifts the whole bra from the front. Normally, I would not let this happen but I am so uninterested that I'm mildly amused. Like all men who view the bosom of life for the first time in person, he pauses to deeply inhale and admire them. They are a full and perky sight to behold and I'm often asked if they are fake. Absolutely not.

He just dives in face first and begins to motorboat, then lick them with his whole tongue! No tip-of-the-tongue action. No licks and nibbles. No sucking. Actual licking like they are giant mounds of chocolate ice cream. STOP! Then out of nowhere – just out of the blue – not even sure which shade of blue, this man licks the entire side of my face with his flat, wet tongue. From chin to temple. This *must* be how baby cheetahs feel when I watch their mothers groom them on Animal Planet. I am paralyzed with confusion because that has never happened before. The most face/tongue action I've ever received was when my newborn niece thought it would be ok to try to nurse on my lower cheek.

That was cute and excusable. This, however, is neither.

When he attempts to revisit the twins, I non-verbally object by putting them back in the house where they belong. And with behavior like that, they will never come out to play with him again!

"Lemme do *the thing*," He says with a smirk while looking down toward my special lady region.

"No thanks, I'm good."

"Come on, lemme *do* it, I've never gotten any complaints. You'll enjoy it."

I can say that every man who has EVER told me that he's never gotten any complaints, needed to get ALL the complaints. But guess what, guys? Contrary to popular belief, we women don't complain about everything. We only bring it up if it's something that we deem fixable and we feel that you're worth the time and effort it takes to repair it. But if the performance is so far beyond mending, it's not worth mentioning ever again. *But, I mean he IS very enthusiastic with that tongue, maybe he'd be ok? Ugh, probably not. He is NO Diego.*

"Here's your water."

I press it to his chest then walk into the living room, take a seat on the couch, and cover back up with my Steelers blanket. Sam follows me in and sits far enough away that he has access to my feet which he begins to carefully massage. Planting kisses up the inside of my leg, continuing up to my inner thigh, this man is relentless in his pursuit to attempt to do "the thing" as he calls it, and I don't know why. What makes a man want to put his mouth on the body of a woman who is so clearly not interested in having it there?

Instead of sliding my bottoms off like any sober person would, Sam feels confident enough to get "the thing" done by sliding the crotch of my boxers to the left, which already tells me that no good will come of this. Every muscle in my face is getting a workout trying to assess what the actual hell he is doing down there. Brows up. Frowning. Cheeks puffed out. Air released. One eye closed. Other eye closed. Mouth pursed to the side. Both eyes *wide* open. I can't. Someone needs to tell this man what a clitoris is, where it's located, what its purpose is in this situation, how to properly stimulate it, and what happens when it's handled correctly. *Then* someone needs to show him *how* to handle it correctly because I have a *day* job! I don't have that kind of *time*! This catastrophe requires prayer, at *least* a semester abroad, and a bottle of Jack because I'm pretty sure he's licking my boxer shorts right now.

I look over at the TV and see that Serena is still on pause, so I reach over for the remote and press play. She is performing way better in this match re-run than he is doing "the thing." I'm not sure how he doesn't notice that the TV is now on, but who cares. The rally between the two ladies is a lengthy and riveting one that has me in suspense to see who is going to get the point. They are playing some serious big babe tennis! So my breathing is becoming slightly erratic because this tension is *killing* me – it's SO good! The match – not his "thing." After the 20-hit rally, Serena misses, the ball goes out of bounds and she loses the point after all that effort. I am so distraught for her that I let out a soft moan-like sigh, at which point Sam pops his head up from between my legs.

"You LIKE that gurl, DON'T 'chu!?"

He then continues doing whatever he seems to *think* is about to finish the job that, unbeknownst to him, never *really* got started. Oh, the indescribable look of shock and utter horror on my face right now. I'm done.

"Yeah, you can stop now."

When someone tells you that you're more than welcome to cease whatever activity *should* be giving them pleasure, feel free to take that as a complaint. But this man will go on about his life continuing to tell women that he's never received any disparagements about his *thing*.

Sam then stands up in front of me and unzips his pants and his petite penis pops out erect. He's looking at me as if to say, "Your turn." For *what*!? I look at it with that face – y'all know the face. I then slide over to the next couch cushion and get up.

"You just spent the last six minutes licking my *blanket*! Put that thing away."

Add to my TO-DO list: Just call Diego already

CHAPTER 12
first rule of fight club

I've owned my home for a few months now and everyone keeps inquiring when the housewarming party is scheduled. Well, anyone who knows me knows that I have zero interest in having a house full of people spilling food and drinks all over my plush new carpeting. So I don't know why they continue to ask. But to appease the masses, I decide to have a small massage party - a gathering in which a group of friends gets together for drinks, games, and girl talk while we each receive a massage. Brie, Ariah, and Neka have RSVP'd along with Jenna, Liza, and Alexis. I'm a bit concerned about Liza being in attendance because, much like myself, my friends have NO filter and once liquor is involved, only the good Lord knows what will exit their mouths. Liza is definitely among my more wholesome friends. I also invited Dani from my current job and Summer from my previous one. None of my Black friends will be on time and Dani will also inevitably be late.

Blaire shows up with a giant duffel full of sheets for my massage table in preparation for the mass of needy, tense women she's about to relax. She enters the gently lit living room scented of Pier One's Vintage Linens. In the dining room is a smorgasbord of various well-placed appetizers spanning the length of the antique mahogany table. In the kitchen, Blaire is excited to see the spread of numerous mixers, wine, and liquor options, along with sexy individualized glassware so the girls can readily identify their drinks. The kitchen smells of hot appetizers ready for consumption.

"Ooooh mamas this looks *great*! What all is on the agenda?"

"Well, I'm thinkin' who doesn't love a game night? So the girls are bringing some of their favorite games, my cable offers karaoke so maybe a little of that, of course some drinks, food, and sillies."

"Sounds like fun, I'm kinda jealous that I'll be downstairs massaging all you heifers," Blaire jokes.

"Now you know damn well you can come up and join in whenever you want."

Blaire goes down to the basement to arrange her workstation just as Liza arrives to see if I need help setting up. I can always count on her to be early. But because I'm so punctual, everything is already done. So instead, we get to sit and catch up before the arrival of the others. We chat for only a few minutes before Summer, Jenna, and Alexis all arrive back to back. After hugs and introductions, everyone migrates straight to the kitchen toward the spirits. Over the next half hour, everyone has arrived and congregated in the kitchen around the liquor, because who cares about food, right? Eventually, we move into the dining room for the apps and then into the living room for games, where I warn them that spillage of any food will result in immediate ejection from the party. These harlots giggle like I'm joking, but my sister Neka knows damn well I'm not because she's the same way with her house.

Time passes as a riveting game of Family Feud progresses. Brie says in her BEST game show Steve Harvey voice, "100 people surveyed, top five are on the board. Lookin' for the numba one ansa' here. Name. The TOP five. Most romantic ways. Couples make love."

Alexis chimes in first, throwing her index finger in the air and loudly screaming, "IN THE BUTT!"

"Wait WHAT!?!?" It was like something out of a movie when you hear the record scratch and all activities cease. Everyone looks at her while laughing hysterically!

"When did that get romantic?" Jenna questions.

"Oooh I'm glad my dude don't be romancin' me like that," Neka jokes. "What happened to candles and rose petals?"

"No more liquor for her! She is cut OFF," one of the girls laughs as she tosses her a bottled water.

"I'm not even drinking," Alexis laughs, shrugging her shoulders.

"Well then that makes your answer even *worse*!" Brie replies with a chuckle. "Sooo, just out of curiosity, you don't have to answer but who here has tried it? Especially if it's as 'romantic' as Alexis says it is!"

Everyone laughs at Brie's sarcastic question while Summer, Jenna, and Lexi slowly raise their hands and everyone looks around.

"Oh don't act like only the white girls like romantic butt stuff," Summer says adamantly! "Come on now!"

All of the other ladies in the room giggle and are silently giving each other the side eye to see who will fess up first and admit to also being intrigued by back-door play. Poor innocent Liza is turning a shade of red that even Crayola doesn't offer in the jumbo box. Finally, Brie gulps her drink and informs the room that she's down for the cause but her husband is too big, at which point multiple women take sips of their drinks.

Neka hops up and says, "It ain't too big, you just gotta know how to position yourself to relax all your shit – no pun intended." We all laugh as she situates herself on the floor in a fetal position.

"Um, excuse me slut muffin, I thought you said you didn't *do* that?" I question in a sassy tone.

"Hey. Don't worry 'bout what my man does wit' all'is! Ok, so the best way to do it is to get on your side and throw this leg up. When we have to do rectals, this is how we position the patients so it must be effective. Y'all let me know – y'all bitches know I don't *do* this!"

We are talking so loudly and laughing so hard that I know this can't possibly be relaxing for the person being massaged directly beneath us. Blaire enters the living room with Ariah to find Neka on the floor with one leg up and her booty tooched out with all the girls around her laughing hysterically. Poor Liza still looks mortified.

"What the hell is happening here? Do we even want to know?" Blaire asks.

"Well, Neka here was showing us the best position in which to try back door love for the first time," Dani tries to state in the most natural and diplomatic fashion possible, which makes us all laugh even harder because first of all, we're tipsy as hell. Secondly, there is nothing natural or diplomatic about my sister gyrating on my living room floor right now, and pardon me for asking but *how* did we go from Family Feud to *this*?

Blaire doesn't seem the least bit shocked by this because she's freakier than all of us combined. "Oh! Well a great rule of thumb, if you can look at his penis and realize you've had bowel movements larger than that, you can absolutely try it with him. So who's next for a massage?" she says ever so casually like she helped pen the Kama Sutra.

"ME! I AM! I'M NEXT. THANK YOU!" Liza says as she damn near does a gold medal Olympic hurdle over the ladies on the floor to get to that basement and away from the lewd conversations taking place.

"She ain't lyin' at all," I say. "That happened to me once! I accidentally had anal sex – a little bit." Everyone is cracking up.

"I know I just walked in and probably missed a lot but how do you *accidentally* have a *little bit* of booty love? You either did it intentionally or you didn't," Ariah says as she pours a drink to join in the madness. "And how the *hell* did y'all get on this *topic*!?" These girls are all gathered around in silence, holding their wine glasses, on pins and needles waiting to hear about this alleged accident.

"Wellll... It was really small... And he was drunk. He thought he was going into the right place but since I was sober, I knew that he wasn't. I was going to stop him but then I thought to myself, ehhh whatever let's just see what happens... and so it happened a little bit."

As I finish that portion of the story, I just see open mouths, presumably in shock.

"I mean the man came to my house with a box of condoms called Snugger Fit. They were so *tiny*, y'all! I didn't even know that was a thing. Did y'all know that was a thing?"

Everyone in the room is dying laughing and Jenna, who is mid-swallow, chokes on her wine because who is expecting to hear that? We've all heard of Magnum condoms for larger men but no one in that room, until today, knew there existed a condom called Snugger Fit tailored especially for the smaller-sized man.

"Bitch you gotta be secure as hell to walk up to the clerk and ask for that shit! Was that Eugene or William?" Ariah asks, not caring about the privacy of either man.

"That was Eugene but he and William could've shared that box cuz li'l Willie swore he was beatin' it up with his itty bitty stuff. Always wanted to know where I was going after we would have sex. Ummm... *home*, fool! So I can orgasm."

"Ope. Well damn," Brie says nonchalantly while sipping on her drink like that's none of her business.

"Wait," Dani says with deep concern. "I don't want to like, offend anyone or anything but were they both... African American?" she whispers.

Those of us who know the guys all nod and look at each other like, why the hell is she whispering?

"Ok, well, so, I thought that... Aren't African American men supposed to have... ya know..." She begins to gesture her hands really far apart and we all start laughing because we know where she is going with that.

"GIRL, NO!"

"I *wish* that was one stereotype that was *true*!"

Objections are chiming in from all of the Black women in the room, and from Jenna.

"Yeah but what about the whole 'once you go Black you never go back' thing?" Summer asks so innocently yet inquisitively. She takes a drink as her bright blue eyes widen while she waits for an answer. We all look at Jenna because, with her curvy sexy physique, thick thighs, and hindquarters, it's just assumed that she's down with the swirl. As the only person in the room who has slept with both white and Black men, she's really the only person absolutely qualified to answer the question. We can say why we *think* Black men make superior lovers, but until we sample the various cookies from the jar, we'll never really know.

"Wait. Why y'all lookin' at *me*?" Jenna asks incredulously.

"Because to *my* knowledge, *we*'ve never had sex with white men. So it's your show boo boo." I pour another glass of wine ready to hear this. I prop myself up and stare at her how all these trollops stare at ME when they're waiting for a story.

"OMG... Ok, well... for *me*, it's not the size stereotype since we've already determined that's not real. It's that... thing they have..."

"That swag..." Brie chimes in assuredly with numerous agreements behind her.

"YES! And the way they move is just different – the rhythm, the way the hips move. Never just in and out, like I can't explain it. There's just so much... effort and intention."

Dani sits fascinated by it all while Summer is just intrigued.

"Wowww... So what you're saying is I need to find a new man?" Summer asks. "I feel like that's what I just heard. 'Cause that doesn't sound like *any* sex *I'm* currently having!"

"I got mine from Belize. Marco's not Black but close enough complexion-wise," Jenna laughs. "And Renée you are lying! You *did* have sex with that white boy!"

They all turn to look at me, shocked, like I've been holding out on them. I am still in the single digits with the number of sexual intercourse partners I have had, so I can say with absolute certainty I have no clue who she is talking about.

"Ahhh yup, college - dude with the coasters," Neka confirms, visibly nodding.

"*That* doesn't *count*!"

"You do understand that when a man inserts his penis into your vagina, *it counts, bitch*!" Clearly, Dani has had too many glasses of wine and my tacky-ass friends are beginning to rub off on her.

"If it doesn't *fit*, and we can't actually *do* it, then it doesn't *count*! And he wasn't just white, he was Cuban too." I clarify as we laugh.

"I have *two* kids!" Dani giggles, "So that man could've fit! What went wrong?"

The evening was innocent enough – I was at Mateo's house finishing our studies for our Gender & Communication exam. To look at his well-decorated home, one would never expect a man with such urban appeal to be its primary resident. When he brought out drinks and sat next to me on the couch, I placed mine on the coaster so as to not ruin his expensive-looking wooden table. He stopped me and asked what I was doing, then informed me that what I intended to set my glass upon was not a coaster. Closer inspection revealed that it was, in fact, a condom. I couldn't tell because the lights had been dimmed.

Wait, they make condoms the size of coasters now? Hold up? They make penises that fit into condoms the size of coasters now? I had to see this monstrosity because, in my mind, there was no way this white boy was about to fill out anything that size. So of course I asked to see it. He looked at me with his smoldering brown eyes, smiled, and agreed. He gestured for me to come closer to him, which I did. Mateo was large and muscular so it was nothing for him to scoop me up and position me on top of him while passionately kissing, still fully clothed. Beneath me, I could feel him and every bit of the growing reason why he owned a condom that large, so I was obligated to take a peek. I felt like I should've photographed it for posterity, or made a mold of it, as it was a stunning sight to behold. But I was so new and had only ever had sex with one person, so his baby elephant trunk would've destroyed my precious lady diamond.

"Your 'precious lady diamond'? What the hell do I keep walking *in* on?" Blaire jokingly asks as she brings Liza back up from her massage. "Who's next?"

No one wants to leave because they don't want to depart from the conversation, but finally, Neka agrees to go next. She chugs the entire glass of wine she just poured and follows Blaire downstairs. Liza reluctantly rejoins the conversation, praying that it's nowhere near as tawdry as it was when she left it. She's going to be disappointed.

"Ooooh, you shoulda just *tried* it," Ariah chimes in.

"Bitch, NO. You're full of bad advice! *You* told me to have sex with Keith's ass!"

"No I didn't!"

"Yes you *did*!" I begin to sarcastically mock her, "Just tryyyy it. You're not feeelin' him but maybe if the sex is good you'll start to liiiike himmm."

"Yeah… you right. I said that dumb shit," she laughs. "It sounded serviceable at the time."

"Well, what happened?" asks Summer, as the rest of the girls giggle.

"So stupid here *does*! Even though I wasn't interested in him romantically, I did it cuz I thought maybe Ariah had a good point. Plus, he was a good guy, very sweet to me, and had potential, but reminded me so much of my father that it was creepy and not a sexual turn-on. But dumb dumb here did it anyway, listening to *her* simple ass! It was a hot mess! His head game was a travesty and he never even got it all the way in!"

The girls begin to laugh and Dani asks, "What does that even *mean*?"

"Look. My womanhood is snug y'all. He had to work his way in and within two partial attempts, he just… whooopsed!"

"STOPPP IT!" Summer exclaims. They are cracking up and my face is stoic and ever so serious because who actually wants to make this up? Not to mention the fact that just thinking about sex ending like that is frustrating in itself.

"So that kinda counts but not really either," Dani jokes. "So when was the last time you had sex with someone for more than two strokes?"

"Little Eugene and that was *years* ago. But it kept coming out so does that count!? I've been celibate for about... ever. Yeah, forever. Swear my lady bits are about to pack up and leave town!"

Yes, I meet a fair amount of men and go on a decent number of dates, but only a handful ever make it beyond a first, and fewer than that any further. So how am I *ever* supposed to get to a sexual relationship? I could just have one-night stands and go on about my day, but even if I were interested, none of them qualify for that either. Besides, sex is very emotional for me, and I find that my body responds better when intimacy is with someone for whom I care deeply. I also tend to form attachments quickly and easily with men who aren't forming them back with me – likely due to those aforementioned "daddy issues." So as a result, I have started to take the wait-and-see approach. I *wait* for all the stupidity to exit his mouth and *see* him talk himself right on out of gettin' these panties.

Because I'm too damn old for this craziness. One guy, who I had yet to ever meet, talked on the phone for *nine* uninterrupted minutes as he basically told me that if I *needed* him to take me out a few times before he could hit it, then that's fine. *No, sir. NOT fine. We quite literally never need to meet.*

"Oh, her lady bits aren't goin' *any*where as long as Diego is around," Alexis says with lust in her eyes. "She hadn't even made an official offer on this house and was tellin' me how she was gonna let him sample her picnic basket!"

"My snack box, bitch!"

"Your *what*!?" Summer asks in total confusion.

"Are you calling your 'Va-Jim-Jam' a snack box?" Dani asks equally confused.

"Are *you* calling my snack box a VA-JIM-JAM!? What the hell *is* that!?" We all laugh.

These poor ladies I work with couldn't have anticipated this kind of information when they were invited to visit my home. Now I need to hope it doesn't end up circulating my current and former workplaces.

Dani continues, "And who is this Diego and why haven't I heard about him at work? He sounds hot! Dieeegooo," she repeats in a sultry voice.

Before I can even get a word out, all of the other girls, except Liza, begin to give a roundabout, yet fairly explicit explanation of Diego's role in my life that is nowhere near appropriate for work without another HR visit. Dani and Summer listen in shock and awe.

"How do I sign up for *that* shit!?" Summer asks jokingly - but I sense she's serious.

"So you have a man who *just* comes to your house *only* to perform cunnilingus and that's it? And then he leaves?" Dani asks bewildered, while everyone else bursts into laughter.

"Yo, did you just say 'cunnilingus'!?" Brie laughs, "We are too damn tipsy to be that proper! I haven't heard that word since eighth-grade sex ed!"

Dani is older, so I am not surprised when she drops the appropriate terminology on us. Nope, that's a lie. I think we all are. Liza finally laughs because as sweet and pure as she is, even she doesn't call it that. After being made fun of for her proper jargon, Dani pulls up an old Saturday Night Live sketch on YouTube about 'Colonel Angus', but the way they say it, it runs together and sounds like 'cunnilingus' with a southern accent. The few who have seen it are already laughing before the hilarious video even begins playing! She declares that Diego shall henceforth be known as "The Colonel."

One by one the ladies finish their massages and the night ends with Neka and Brie showing us all how to properly twerk since they have *all* the stacks in the back. So sad. Neither Liza nor I have enough booty meat to twerk and make it look sexy. The remaining ladies who do, either have no rhythm or are not genetically predisposed to be able to move their pelvises in that manner. And Dani is *convinced* she can twerk like the sistas, so she is determined to participate.

As the ladies sober up, the size of the gathering slowly dwindles. I then have to let these chicks know that this shit is like Vegas! What happens at the massage party, *stays* at the massage party. There is a code! This shit is like the first rule of Fight Club! I don't expect to hear a damn thing about anything that went on here because bitch, you were never here.

Add to my TO-DO list: Nothing because this shit never happened

CHAPTER 13
what about my needs?

DING DING

Hassan: I'm down your way, you care if I stop by?
Renée: It's fine...

I have nothing else to do this Saturday afternoon, so why not. Hassan is still trying to work his way back into my good graces after that shoveling incident. Little does he know that my graces aren't that good and they're like Fort Knox once you're out. I get tired of constantly allowing men second, third, and fourth chances after doing dumb mess they know they shouldn't have done in the first place.

I quickly straighten up the house a bit and make myself somewhat more presentable since he doesn't live that far away. From my bedroom window, I see his little red Nissan pull up and he emerges with a bag of what looks like takeout. *Aww how sweet! And it just so happens I'm hungry.* I make my way downstairs to see that he is already perched atop my porch ledge with a pair of chopsticks going to town.

As I step outside while putting the finishing touches on my messy bun, he smiles and nods at me with a mouth full of noodles.

"Dang, you couldn't even wait for me, huh? That hungry?"

He gives me a funny look so I give him one back as I look into the very *empty* paper bag that is sitting in the chair beside him.

"Wait, did you for real just stop for food on the way to *my* house and not bring any for *me*? Like not even some shrimp fried rice!? Like for *real*!? It's $6.50. I have a five, a one, and two quarters in the house right now if it's that much of a stretch for you."

"Well, it was a last-minute decision to stop."

"You have a phone."

"I didn't think you'd want any. You're on a diet."

"I still have to EAT!" I exclaim with hunger and annoyance.

"Well, you can have some of mine. It's chicken," he says, munching away.

Is it though? But regardless of what meat he's eating, it's so incredibly tacky to arrive at someone's house with food for *only* oneself. I would *never* show up at my friends' homes with lunch without a call first. Liza lives near all the great eateries and when I plan to stop at one before visiting her home, I always check to see if she, her hubby, or my niece want anything. If they say no, then cool, but they know I'm coming with yummies for me – don't be all up in my plate. And in this situation, if this is how Hassan is trying to regain my affection, he absolutely gets an "F." This only highlights how thoughtless he is regarding a woman's wants, needs, and feelings.

"I don't *want* yours. What I *want* is my $6.50 shrimp fried rice."

He sits on my ledge still chewing like he doesn't see how his actions are horribly inconsiderate. Much like when he invited me to *his* work carnival the previous summer and I paid for all of the rides we rode. One would think that he would at least cover the slice of pizza we had for lunch and maybe the cotton candy. But if one thought *that*, then one would be thinking far too highly of him.

I leave him on my ledge with his noodles to go in to make myself a turkey and pepper jack sandwich with some Sour Cream & Cheddar Baked Lays on the side. By the time I finish my not-so-Master Chef-worthy creation, he has finished his meal and is gathering his trash to toss.

Stepping onto the porch with my plate, I notice that there is a line of cars at the stop sign in front of my house. In the thickness of this traffic is a clean, merlot-colored Dodge Challenger with fully tinted windows that catches my eye. It's one of my dream cars, but since I still don't have kids, I shop sensibly so I don't have to try to put an infant in a two-door muscle car. That poor baby would end up all concussed with me accidentally knocking its head off the side of the car trying to get it in and out of the car seat.

The passenger window rolls down like I've been caught peeking, so I squint to see who's inside. Would you look at that! Diego finally got a car – a nice ass one too! He smiles, glances over to Hassan, then back to me, and shoots a look as if to say, "Who's *this* little cornball?" I shoot him back a turned-up nose look that basically says, "No one important." He smirks, nods, licks his sexy lips, and rolls up his window. I'm sure he'll be back soon and I can't wait.

As I sit in one of the chairs across from the ledge with lust likely slathered all over my face, Hassan boldly says to me, "So you got anything sweet in there for dessert?"

Blank stare. *I quit.*

♀ ♂ ♀ ♂

So finally, a date I am excited about! Dinner with my boo, Ariah. I know I jokingly said earlier I was her man and whatnot, but I have a mortgage now, so we're going Dutch tonight. We always meet in a great part of town that is equidistant from us so we can drink, shop, eat, drink some more... Hey, work is stressful!

I can see her towering over everyone in the waiting area as she enters the restaurant. This tall, stately creature rocking her mini afro stomps the hall like she's stomping the runway in her infamous bitch-kicker boots like she's coming to handle business. Thank heavens I'm on her good side tonight. She leans in to hug me because she knows it's happening and has come to accept it. But if it were up to her, there would be a secret handshake that didn't involve touching, eye contact, or any in-person interaction.

The restaurant is quickly filling so we try to keep our voices down while we laugh and cackle like two kids finally together for recess. We've officially had enough drinks that we find it entertaining to tie cherry stems into knots with our tongues, so some of the things we're *now* catching up on are probably best left for phone conversations and not public ears. Ariah reaches into her purse for her phone which has been vibrating all evening.

"Everything ok?" I ask.

"Yeah girl, just this dude I been kiiinda talkin' to but not really. He drives for Uber but wanted me to drive all the way across town to see him. No."

As she continues to describe this hot mess of a man and a few of his other outlandish requests, it's all sounding very familiar to me.

"Is his name BJ? Just be at the bar chillin' & stuff?"

Ariah squints her dark brown eyes at me, "Yesss. All the *time*! But how do YOU know him?"

"THAT'S THE CHICKEN DUDE!!" I shout! "You remember! The chicken dude!"

Like saying it twice in a row verbatim would actually jog her memory. This same guy met me for fro-yo and was later telling me about this amazing chicken spot that he liked to frequent and take wings over to his mother. So I asked him how could I get on the chicken list because damn, girlie likes good chicken too! He told me those wings were expensive! So I'm thinking, hey, I'm a good woman, surely I'm worth the price of some delicious poultry. He then goes on to tell me that they're $15/dz. But if I buy mine, he will bring them to me. When I inquired what would happen when we finally went on a *real* date, he told me that he would pay for his and I would pay for my own. Ok. You go enjoy your mama and that chicken because you two will make a lovely couple. I don't think it's unreasonable to expect a man to pay for a first date. I have no problem taking my man out and treating him to nice meals and gifts, but if it's too much of a financial imposition to get some damn chicken, then *you* need to find someone else to date. And I can promise you, Ariah will not be the one. Hell, she likes chicken too!

Ariah sat stunned as we showed each other text messages he was sending to her and inbox messages he was sending to me on the dating app.

"So now what?" she asks, feeling awkward about us both talking to the same man that really neither of us wants.

"Oh, we 'bout to take this selfie together to post on my dating profile so he can see us together lookin' dead into the camera at his triflin' ass! I wish I had some chicken!"

All this sexy melanin and natural curls poppin', we are working these camera angles like we are battling it out for America's Next Top Model. I immediately upload this selfie, chock full of exotic eyes and pouty lips, as the main photo on the app so as soon as he goes in again, he will see our sexy faces - together. I also upload it to social media to let people know we were out here being #petty. But if men weren't out here acting so #stupid, this could all be #avoided.

"So. Now that that's done. Are we splittin' dessert or what?"

"Bitch, you *know* I'm on a diet," Ariah snaps.

"What the hell's your point? You're *always* on a diet."

Ariah silently stares at me, purses her lips, crosses her hands in prayer, and looks deep in thought then deeply inhales.

"Yeah... You right. I'mma get this cheesecake."

That weirdness is why I love Ariah. While we enjoy dessert, I slide my phone across the table so she can read this thread of messages from Eli. This would be the same man who wanted me to borrow a truck from *another* man to help him move a table. Yeah, see no. You need to cultivate some male friends here, buddy.

Eli: Hey What are you doing?

Renée: Client work

Eli: Come over, you can work here. I'm working too.

Renée: Oh you got furniture finally?

Eli: No.

Renée: ??? So where am I supposed to do my work?

Eli: On the floor

Renée: Are you crazy!? Why would I leave my comfortable workspace to come do my work on your FLOOR?

Eli: Well when I came to your place we just sat around. We were on the porch.

Renée: Right cuz even my PORCH has furniture!!

Eli: So ur not coming then?

Renée: That would be a no. Call me when you have furniture.

"And no! Don't look at me with those eyes like I'm being all over the top here. This man has a career and a BMW. He has a side hustle in real estate and owns multiple homes, some that are rented, others that are flipped for sale. He can *afford* furniture. He's just bein' cheap and don't wanna buy any since he'll only be here for two years."

"Well damn, two years is a long ass time to not have a couch!"

"Girl. When I *did* finally visit, he still didn't have any, just a blow-up mattress in the living room. I asked him, 'You just gon keep it like this?' and he was like 'Yup I got the bed and the TV here so it's cool.' I asked why he wouldn't just put it in the bedroom, but he said he liked it where it was so hey... Not my apartment, not my problem. If he likes it, I love it."

"So he *did* have a bedroom? It wasn't like a studio." I shake my head no. "Then what was in the bedroom?" Ariah asks.

"A stuffed deer head. On the floor."

"YOU ARE LYYYING RIGHT NOW!!"

"OMG. Why would I make that *up*!? Shit, I was just as surprised as *you*! But I guess he'll always have some head in his bedroom."

"Ooooh! Scandalous! Check please!" She laughs while gathering her wallet to prepare to pay her bill.

♀ ♂ ♀ ♂

Instead of taking the steps to work off that cheesecake, we lazily opt for the escalator to head downstairs to the toy store in the mall. Not toys for our sweet nieces and nephews, toys for US. Ariah just wants a new one and I am tired of buying batteries, so surely I can find something that's rechargeable.

Standing in front of this expansive wall of sex apparatus and apparel is making me think of Diego's freaky proclivities. He would love nothing more than to see me bound in this thick, sturdy four-point restraint system and gagged so I can't scream "NO MORE" while uselessly attempting to fight him off of my exhausted body. He literally doesn't understand that sometimes too much pleasure is just *too much*. I'm only human! I need my oxygen levels to return to normal so I don't pass out! Then my eyes slowly wander over to the anal toys, which Diego is also open to exploring. Mine, not his - he made that abundantly clear. The vibrating black plug intrigues me but I came here for...

"Bitch get out the butt section! I mean... Unless... You uhh... Tryin' to uhh..."

"No, not today," I laugh as we scooch a few feet over to the mini-pleasure section. "Ooh this one plugs in!"

"Oh, you just *tryin* to get electrocuted, huh?"

"Well, you're supposed to unplug it first. Right?" We laugh.

"You need a *man-sized* toy," she says, pulling the giant red one down from the shelf. "That thing is gonna close up if you don't use it soon! I know it's been at *least* a year; why don't you just have sex with Diego already?"

"Well, first of all, don't call her 'it' - my beautiful precious va-gem stone is a lady." Ariah is rolling her eyes and shaking her head. "And secondly, it's been closer to three years. And lastly, we already discussed what happened *last* time you told me to 'just sleep with someone.' I'm not listening to *that* shit again! Besides, I don't *trust* Diego enough to sleep with him even though... OMG, it would probably be so bomb."

"As much as you lecture me about STDs, why would you let him put his mouth on *her* if you don't trust him enough to have real sex?"

"I'm entitled to make one bad decision. I overthink *every*thing else. And shit, I haven't had actual sex in ages! Let me have my one bad but *very* pleasurable decision please."

Under any other normal circumstance, none of this would have ever occurred. There is no other man from my past whom I have continually been intimate with, on any level, that I didn't trust. I was also always in relationships with or seriously dating them as well. But I can't even date Diego because I just don't trust him. For some unknown reason, he rarely looks me in the eyes when we talk and he is seldom able to be honest with me, so as a result I assume he's lying about everything, like so many others I encounter. I really just want to tell them all to ask themselves the following six questions before total bullshit falls out of their mouths:

1. Is the person I'm about to lie to smarter than me?

2. Have I interacted with this person enough that they can likely spot the lie I'm telling?

3. Has this person caught me in a lie before?

4. Does this person I'm about to lie to have ANY basic common sense?

5. Would I be angry if this person lied to ME?

6. Do I even remotely care about this person?

If no, then lie on, brotha. But if they've answered yes to any of the above - TELL THE DAMN TRUTH! There's a novel idea... But alas, it never happens.

There are many instances in which I'm sure Diego is being honest, but I wouldn't believe him if he were. That would make for a very toxic relationship. That wouldn't matter much because he doesn't seem to be able to stay faithful in one of those anyway. And though I've never lied to him, *ever*, I also feel like he doesn't completely trust me either, which is insane when I've only ever displayed honesty. Some of that trust issue possibly has to do with the fact that Diego has always held a strong disdain for Tyce, even though we've only ever been just friends. I'm not sure if it's because Diego feels like his hood mentality can't compete with a highly educated, white-collar man or because he's unable to be "just friends" with a woman so he assumes that no man can. Therefore, in his mind, me and Tyce *must* be doin' the deed? Not sure, but either way, I weigh the pros and cons of everything I do. All of my actions have reactions and consequences, so I am well aware that Ariah is making the most valid point ever.

"You *enjoy* yourself, girl! Let that bad decision eat off your freaky li'l lunch tray!"

"It's my snack box, Bitch! Damn!" We both laugh.

"Whatever. I don't understand it. I'm not into it all like that – just gimme the D," Ariah proclaims.

"That's because no one's ever *done* it right. As soon as someone chomps that box the *right* way, mark my words, you *will* call me, no matter the time. Well... as soon as you recover your liver function... and your vision corrects... and your extremities regain sensitivity... and you can form full sentences again. *Then* you will call me and tell me all about it."

Ariah is standing entranced, mouth ajar, holding a colossal red dildo in her hand under her chin, "Wowww... And Diego does all that to you?"

I remove two 19-speed, USB-powered bullets from the wall and walk up to Ariah, smile sweetly, and say softly, "Mmmmmm hmm... with just his mouth. Here, buy this one. It doesn't need batteries." I hand it to Ariah so she can put back the weapon of vaginal destruction she's holding so we can check out with the 8Oish-year-old male clerk. He just smiles as he slowly rings up our purchases. *Awkward.*

Next stop, shoes. It would be unnatural to visit a mall and not swing by every shoe store, though this one is unusually packed today. That Buy One, Get One Half Off will do it every time. Unfortunately, I don't see anything I like to split the cost with Ariah, but she sees enough that she should be able to take advantage of the sale. We have such vastly different taste. Her style looks so good on her. But if I raided her closet, I would look like a total wackadoodle. She complains about needing a pedicure while trying on too many pairs of shoes, so I figure, hell, might as well see what all this "new little friend" has to offer. All of the seats are in use by customers, so I lean against the wall and discreetly read the package.

- 19 different vibration settings
- Waterproof for enjoyment in the bath or shower
- Perfect for couples or individual use
- USB charging cable included

"Well damn," I whisper to her. "This is waterproof!"

"If you don't put that thing away! There are children here!" she hisses back.

Fine. I do, but Ariah is taking so long that I'm getting bored, so I pull it back out and open the package just to see it – and maybe check out the instructions so I have a head start. Knowledge is power, but hopefully, *this* thing is *more* powerful! I pull the little plastic tab out that's keeping it from accidentally activating, you know, just to see. But my curiosity gets the better of me so I press the button – just to SEE! It's small enough that it fits in my fist so I can gauge its power on the different settings and no one will even know, right? Wrong. Oh. So. Incredibly. Wrong.

In the palm of my hand, uncharged, on its lowest setting, this 2.5" of silicone magic sounds like a small blender! My eyes widen when I realize how damn strong this thing is - *hot damn*! But shit, Ariah can clearly hear it from just over four feet away.

So I press the button again thinking it will turn off. I never got to the instructions; I have no idea how to actually *work* the thing yet! With a second button push, it goes to a stronger, thus louder version of the previous setting. Ariah's bulging eyes now match the size of mine as she looks around to see if this is as noticeable to the rest of the customers in the store. She quickly deduces that it is by the side eyes and looks of disdain we're getting from the lady on the adjacent bench.

"OMG, turn it off," she whispers through clenched teeth.

"I'm trying!" Every time I hit the button, a new and louder vibration occurs. As I click through, I'm thinking that once I get to the end it will just stop. Still wrong. I begin to crack up laughing because now there is a Morse code of loud, pulsing vibrations happening – and there are *nineteen* settings! More and more heads begin to pop up to investigate down our row, with confused faces trying to figure out what exactly is making that erratic sound. Half the store is crowding around each other watching to see how this plays out.

Ariah desperately jumps up with one red platform sandal on and quickly hobbles over to assist with getting this little buzzing bastard to shut off. I hold it close to my chest while still pressing the button, hoping that the bosom of life can help muffle the rhythmic whirring sounds. It somehow seems to be making everything worse because I accidentally pressed it to the hard plastic casing from which I removed it! *I know I hit this thing nineteen times already*! She leans in close, pressing her girls against mine in an effort to encase the noise while we are fumbling with this tiny little device. I'm certain we look like two lady lovers who just can't wait to get home to try our new love toys. While frantically scuffling to try to end the cadenced love beats as some now traumatized child looks on, Ariah decides to try holding the button down. *Why didn't I think of that?* It works!

Ariah pants heavily and steps back looking at me like an annoyed mother, on a tilt, of course, because she still only has on one platform shoe. She holds out her hand in a very Claire Huxtable-esque manner.

"Give me the toy," she demands flatly.

I stand in front of her looking like a child being publicly chastised for opening a bauble that Mother expressly said *not* to play with. Oh wait, that's what's actually happening. I obediently hand her my new toy.

"And the package. And the bag."

I comply.

"Now sit HERE," she says sternly and points to the seat that was once hers to try on shoes.

As the cashier and others in the aisle look on, I purse my lips to the right and bite the inside of them and sit down as Ariah hurriedly removes her one red shoe, gathers her things, and readies to leave the store to forego the BOGO sale. This is probably the last time Ariah will ever shop with me, but I'm just saying, *damn* she is gonna *love* that bullet!

Add to my TO-DO list: Find a new shoe store because I can NEVER come back here

CHAPTER 14

porch playtime, the sequel

"What are you up to?" Liza asks when I answer my ringing phone.

"I am in the process of re-tiling the ceiling in the guest room. Thanks to Ariah, I ended up with hundreds of dollars of drop ceiling tiles to sexify this room."

"You're doing that all by yourself?"

"Why do you sound so shocked? It's not like I have a man to help. Looks good so far though – can't wait for you to see it!"

"Well, what happened to Al? He probably coulda helped with – oh, never mind. I forgot you seem to attract the *least* helpful men alive."

"Girl, right!? Besides, Al can't help me with *my* house because he needs to stay home and focus on his *own* damn horror show he calls a house. I was afraid to cough because I thought the thing would fall over."

"Ohhh, well that's... not good," Liza says with sweet concern.

Al came to visit me after a few dates. We hit the Redbox and popped some corn to enjoy a movie night. The entire evening and every time we had seen each other prior to that, he was always sniffling, but it was that repulsive, phlegm-filled swine kind of snorting, where it's very clear that all of the thick nasal mucus was being swallowed, which is absolutely disgusting. He insisted that he didn't have a cold and that it was probably just allergies, but with my germophobic nature, I wanted no parts of anything happening in his mouth because I didn't want to catch whatever it was that he claimed he didn't have.

After visiting my bathroom, he commented on what a beautiful home I had and that he was nervous to show me his. That concerned me because I am terribly anal about my surroundings and could never envision spending my life with someone incapable of keeping house. Somehow, he wasn't ashamed enough because he surely invited me over.

Remember the door from the movie The Color Purple? The one that Mister kicks open? It's made of a wood perimeter with some screen attached that doesn't actually close? That's the door that was on this man's house when we entered. The actual door somehow didn't close completely and there were spaces and gaps along the top and bottom. It also didn't appear as though the deadbolt lined up correctly. The window on the ground level had been broken because he got locked out and needed to get back in. He never got it fixed so anyone could just come into the house if they so desired. He lived deep in the hood, so needless to say, I did not feel safe surrounded by broken doors and windows.

Al began to show me around his home, starting in a kitchen that looked clean-ish at first glance. Meaning the dishes were put away, there was no mess on the stove and very little clutter around, but after standing and just observing for a few minutes while we talked, it was evident that the walls have probably never been cleaned in the twenty years that he had been at that residence. I could see where there once was a clock on the wall because that spot was very clean compared to the surrounding walls. Not everyone knows this because they actually clean, but when food is fried often, oil residue begins to accumulate on the walls and if never removed, dust begins to gather on top of the greasy scum. That was the entire kitchen. Neat but not clean.

He then took me upstairs and I have no idea why because if the rest of the house looked anything like that kitchen, I was going to need a hazmat suit. Apparently, there was a roof issue that caused a huge leak. It looked like black mold was forming throughout the hallway and spreading up the stairs, but he assured me that it wasn't because the roofer said so. How about hiring a new roofer? Or better yet, let's just call the mold remediator and let *him* tell you for sure that this creepy satanic growth is not mold. I tried to hold my breath, but after realizing that no air was circulating through the house, it was pointless. I'm inhaling the black death and that's that.

Once upstairs, he showed me the bathroom where he reached up and twisted the exposed bulb to the right to turn on the light. What the hell happened to the light switch? And why do you not feel compelled to get that shit fixed? *Also,* what happens when you get out of the shower and the light's been on for a length of time and it's really hot? He showed me the designated washcloth that he kept on the dirty sink to turn the light out when it's hot. Sadly, but unsurprisingly, the rest of the bathroom matched that filthy sink. I would say it looked like two men lived there, but that would be insulting to all the grown men who know how to clean their homes. At that point, I no longer needed to use the bathroom – my bladder packed up and said, bitch I will wait for you in the *car*!

I was then led to his master bedroom where the white door was completely black about six inches above and below the actual door knob, which I imagine came from too many years of never cleaning or disinfecting the door. In fact, all of the doors upstairs were white with dirty blackness around the door knobs. So yeah, I was certain that I wanted to touch nothing in that house. He opened the door to show me his bedroom which contained another broken window and a dresser that had open drawers with unfolded clothes just hanging out of them like they were trying in vain to crawl away. It was a hazardous maze to even walk through the room because there was so much random crap littering the floor. And to top it off, the bed, which is usually a focal point of any bedroom, was an unmade disaster. There wasn't a sheet or pillowcase that matched each other let alone the worn-out comforter, which had mostly slumped onto the floor. There was no way that I would lay my naked body down on that bed or would want to take any of my clothes off in that room. I would genuinely fear that something would crawl up inside me and *die*!

He then showed me the guest room which was in total disarray, full of random stacked items, and could've starred in season four, episode ten of Hoarders. There was a giant hole in the ceiling that he said needed to be repaired from that roof leak *four* years ago. At the point where I was looking up at this gaping hole overhead, there was nothing that could convince me that this man had not been breathing black mold for a very long time and that's why all of his constant coughing and sniffling was occurring. The damage was literally *that* extensive.

I was working *so* hard to control my face. But really I just wanted out of the house because I didn't feel safe at all knowing I was breathing in the mold and that at any given time, this very insecure home could be penetrated by anyone who knew how to climb through a window or move aside a few planks of wood and screen. It would take no huffing or puffing to blow this bitch down; an unexpected hiccup would probably suffice. I mean, there could literally be someone hiding in a closet or in that pigsty of a guest room right *now* and we wouldn't know for days.

We headed back downstairs to watch a movie at which time I was given the option to pick a couch because there were three of them. Not sure why anyone needs three couches, but they were all there in the cluttered fire hazard that he called a living room. Candles were also lit to cover a weird scent that was emanating from the dining room. Not sure if it was more mold or something much worse, but midway through the movie, my throat began to get scratchy and I started coughing and sniffling. I knew I didn't have a cold when I arrived. That was my cue to leave his residence because I had no doubt that that black mold was beginning to affect me. Oddly enough, halfway home, my breathing began to improve, so my issues had to have been environmental, much like his. He was in denial.

I could only giggle to myself when Al invited me over the next week to spend the night and watch movies in his bedroom. He even offered to cook for me. No way was that ever going to happen. I felt like if I took my clothes off in that house I would leave with a rash, a smidge of hepatitis, and in need of a tetanus shot!

"Oh wow," Liza says in shock. "So yeah, you're probably better off handling that on your own. I've neglected *my* house some but that story is making me want to get on top of some things ASAP."

"Well glad I could help," I laugh.

♀ ♂ ♀ ♂

Finally, after a long day of beautifying the guest room, all I want to do is sit out on my porch by the fire and relax. Even after a hot shower, my entire body still aches. Not from doing the work, but from falling down nine of my thirteen steps admiring said work. I wanted to see what it would look like from the vantage point of someone coming up the stairs, so I kept backing up until I accidentally backed my happy ass down those stairs. It still hurts to breathe, which means I likely have a rib out of place, but Dr. Jake can pop that right back where it belongs.

Despite my clumsiness, the ceiling looks so sophisticated, even though currently the room is only for show. Just stand and admire it. No touchies, and certainly no sleepies on my pristine white sheets.

I get set up in my regular spot on the porch with my blanket, both phones, water, and snacks – no fire table though. It hasn't cooled down enough yet, so I opt for lighting the eight strategically placed citronella candles instead since mosquitos tend to view me as their personal all-you-can-eat buffet. The entire porch is aglow and looks like I'm either about to summon the satanic forces or sacrifice a virgin – no good can come of either.

One of the most enjoyable parts of sitting on my porch is watching all of the passersby in their cars. Sounds boring, but it's quite riveting. Will they actually stop at the stop sign? How many will be going the wrong way down my one-way street? Yesterday, I watched a passenger in the line of stopping cars open the door and vomit. He closed the door and they kept driving like nothing happened. The week prior, I watched a drunk driver smash into the side of my neighbor's parked car! She was so intoxicated that she got out of her car and simply walked *into* the first house she saw and sat on the steps. So far today, I've seen a grown man sucking his thumb, another man get out of his car and *bark,* and I am appalled at how many people pick their noses at stop signs.

As the sun sets and the traffic dies down creating a much quieter atmosphere, a familiar Merlot vehicle stops at the sign. Upon realizing that I'm porch-timing alone, he decides to park – slowly and badly. How can he own a car that sexy yet can't park it? Diego approaches my porch wearing only a sexy smirk, a black wife beater, dark denim, distressed jeans, and black Timbs. His rippling arms with one full sleeve of ink are exposed and look even more chiseled under the moonlight and flickering of the candles. Someone please call poor Larry and tell him that THIS is how you wear a wife beater.

"Took you long enough to park that beast."

"Haa you got jokes, I see. So this a romantic li'l set up. You spectin' company?" he asks with his thick accent and a tinge of jealousy.

"Yup. The borough's mosquito population will be here within the hour."

"Mmmm... tha's cuz you got that *sweet* sweet," Diego says, smirking and licking his lips.

Sigh... "There's stuff to drink in the mini-fridge in the corner if you're thirsty." I always have to change the subject to take his mind off of the naughty, but it usually goes right back.

"Yo! Fa REAL!? You got a fully stocked fridge out this bitch now? Where I live they would just steal tha whole damn porch. You come out here there jus' be a sidewalk n shit left."

"Yeah, so remind me to never visit *you* then," I joke.

Hours pass while Diego and I catch up and discuss randomness illuminated by only the candlelight. We both toss back a few drinks and enjoy each other's company and conversation. Beyond his special oral skills and outside of the trust issues, Diego has always been someone interesting to just talk to about any and everything. He has so many interesting views on most topics and his conspiracy theories are always debate-worthy. We make each other laugh, which I love because when he does, his hard exterior just melts away and it's totally adorable. We cut up and drink for hours until we realize it's almost 2 a.m. I have no plans to turn in yet, but Diego gets up and begins to blow out my candles one by one and darkness creeps across the porch.

"What are you doing?"

"Blowin' out'cha candles. I'm hungry. Time for that porch picnic."

I look at him in shock, which he likely can't see since he's blown out the majority of the lighting and all that's left is the soft luminescence of the adjacent street light.

"Oh, you're crazy as hell. There is no way that is actually happening with *you* outside on this porch! I was *joking* about a porch picnic."

"I'm not," he counters as he swiftly blows out the last remaining flame on the small table beside me.

Dropping suddenly to his knees in front of me, Diego is only partially concealed by the porch's wall and ledge from anyone walking or driving past the house. He runs his sizeable hands up my soft, exposed thighs and surprisingly gently spreads my legs. He's normally so much more assertive. He doesn't break eye contact with me the entire time which makes me simultaneously uncomfortable and aroused. I inhale to object but very little comes out once he plants his soft lips upon my inner thigh. However, I manage to muster up a few faint words.

"You can't *do* this out here. People are gonna hear."

"Then you need ta cum quieter. Shhhh... Silencio," he whispers with a smirk.

Did this man just shhh me? Diego knows damn well that the result of his work is loud and violent. There has never been a quiet orgasm that involved him, even though I've always tried diligently – especially when my doors and windows are open. Any other man could service me fine out here and people walking by would be none the wiser – guess that doesn't say much for their overall skill levels.

"These are pretty sexy," he says regarding my deep-magenta lace Victoria's Secret panties.

I'm in a semi-erotic daze staring into his sharp hazel eyes until I feel him rip the lace in half and damn near off my body. REALLY!?

"DIEGO! That was a $25 pair of panties! You could've just slid them *down*! What the fuck!?" I angrily whisper.

I'm steadily whisper-yelling at him about his poor decision-making abilities so he smacks my upper, outer thigh then bends around and kisses it to shut me up. Yeah, that works a little. As he works his way toward the front, I begin to object *again* to his chosen location for this current round of who knows how many. My objections are truly half-hearted, so they are barely noted and Diego knows that this IS on my bucket list. Still, I can't help but be concerned.

My protests are silenced as soon as his mouth touches my secret smorgasbord, thus I completely forget any and all grievances and I no longer need to speak to the manager. Though it's dark on the porch, the corner street light is still on and anyone paying attention can tell there are people on it. So as much as I *want* to close my eyes, throw my head back in ecstasy, and let it all out, I have to attempt to control my vocalizations and keep my head on a swivel in case I need to stop him.

The moaning becomes way more audible when he does this thing that I've been trying to figure out forever. It's so delicate and gentle – maybe some sort of sucking with simultaneous tongue flickers, and I feel like it somehow involves teeth, but I really can't tell. Whatever it is, it drives me *senseless* and renders me breathless when I cry out in fierce pleasure, expending all of the air from my body. I grab onto the arms of the chair, though I don't know how much more pressure they can sustain. Diego tightly holds my arms onto the chair, in essence restraining me because he's been doing this long enough to know when I'm about to lose it. We also both know that the way my body reacts to his oral stimulations, I will fuck this *whole* porch up, so restraint is simply a necessary evil!

I yell for him to stop because I can't take the body annihilating pleasure anymore. I'm unable to escape him because I'm seated against a wall with my wrists still restrained. With his broad muscular body positioned between my legs, I'm rendered relatively immobile from the waist down as well. All I can do is hope that Diego has enough compassion to stop before my kidneys begin to fail or something equally crazy!

Still breathing *quite* heavily, which hurts from my earlier trip down the steps, I implore, "Are you gonna let me go now?"

He stares intently at me and smirks while still maintaining a firm grasp on my wrists. I know what that means.

"Oh no no no, you are DONE," I frantically whisper. "There are cars still passing. That was super risky... and *loud*. And you *know* the police drive by all the – AAAHH!"

He starts going again, but my entire body is still tingling from the first round. So everything below my Mason-Dixon line is *extra* sensitive right now. Still being unable to fully relax and let go is helpful right now when I notice Gabriel's two porch lights turn on and illuminate the far end of my porch closest to his. Fortunately, we're on the opposite end and still cloaked by darkness.

"STOP STOP STOP!" I beg seriously and hastily, each "stop" going up another octave, but he doesn't. "The neighbor's lights turned on! I think he's coming out," I murmur.

Diego pauses, peeks up at me, glances over my quivering, bare thigh toward the neighbor, and smiles with pride like he did such an amazing job that the townsfolk had to gather to acknowledge and admire his work. We stare at his porch, Diego in amusement and me in paralyzed horror, as the door opens and Gabriel slowly steps onto the porch.

"Don't move. He's older, so if we don't move, he probably won't *see* us," I whisper. "Like a T-Rex."

Gabriel walks to the front steps to look left and right down the block. He then turns toward my porch but doesn't appear to see us, Diego crouched down and me still seated, both stiff like scared baby bunnies. Except Diego thinks this is amusing and starts kissing my defenseless lower lips again, but I can't move or *say* anything that will risk us being discovered. I do my best to remain still and quiet, which there has never in life been a more formidable task. I'm panting and trembling in an effort to hold back a scream, and if I bite down any harder on my bottom lip, I may require stitches. I pray there is enough hardware holding this porch together because I really don't want to have to explain the pending devastation to a contractor.

Finally, after what feels like hours later, Gabriel stretches and mercifully decides that he has had enough of the fresh, midnight air and lazily ambles back into the house, which means I can finally exhale audibly. His porch lights turn off, which makes Diego pick up his oral pace as he grasps me more tightly against his flickering tongue, forcing me to surrender and cry out in a foreign language I didn't even realize I knew.

By the time it's all said and done, I have no clue how many times I've climaxed, but it's enough that the other chair is tipped over, the mini table has been cleared of all its contents - candles, snacks, drink, cigar and ashes – all on the floor. The worst part is that the gas fire table somehow got overturned and now there is fire glass all over the porch. That's a lie, it wasn't "somehow." I flipped that bitch somewhere around orgasm number four when I managed to escape Diego's taut grasp. So now the porch is a mess, I'm a mess, and Diego? No mess, he just seems satiated with all the damage he's just inflicted on my home and my body.

"That was interestin'. Should be enough ta put'chu ta sleep now though. Go ta bed. I'll be by in the mornin' ta help you clean all'is shit up. Oh an' here."

He reaches into his pocket and drops a fifty-dollar bill into my mailbox.

"For the panties. Get two. That way I don't gotta hear your mouth when I rip 'em off again." He casually takes a swig of his blue Gatorade, leans in, lingers at my lips for a few seconds, smirks, then passionately kisses me goodbye.

My eyes widen in shock watching Diego walk to his car while I sit here feeling so incredibly dirty that that entire verbal exchange really just turned me on. I need a cold shower and my bed... and as soon as my legs work again, I will do that.

I stumble down the stairs after waking from a *really* good sleep thanks to the late-night raiding of the snack box by Diego. I slept until just after 10:00, which is really late for me. As I unchain and unlock the door, I pause and remember the horrible mess that I have to clean up before I can even enjoy my breakfast. That porch was left a wreck and I never want to be looked upon as the trashy-house neighbor. I run back upstairs and throw on some shorts to go out and fight the good fight.

Breathing deeply, I open the door and step out onto the porch with the broom.

"Oh my gosh!"

The porch has been completely put back together – all the fire glass is back in the upright fire table and all the mess that was made has been cleaned. I go into the mailbox to grab that fifty I forgot last night and there is another paper in there – a note that simply reads, "😊, D." He's a man of few written words but damn can he clean. *I'mma need for him to come back here and handle these dishes right quick though*!

As the sun rises over the back of the house and shines on the front of my freshly landscaped lilies, I get comfy in my usual spot on the porch and think about Diego's thoughtful gesture. Since none of my muscles have recovered enough to stand and prepare a proper breakfast at my stove, lazy woman's breakfast it is – a full bowl of Reese's Puffs and a banana. I close my eyes to enjoy the cool morning breeze which takes me back to last night's many moments of ecstasy and a sleazy smile crosses my face. But then, alarming sounds of viciousness jolt my eyes open. It's Sadie losing her entire shit because she sees me on the porch and that is not nearly close enough to where she would like me to be. Is this better than being awakened by my neighbor's love noises? Still up for debate. Gabriel unhands her leash, and Sadie runs full speed to my porch to jump on me, almost spilling my bowl of milk. Of course, I'm the weirdo who eats the cereal and leaves the milk. Eventually, she simmers down as Gabriel takes the open seat on the other side of the fire table.

I'm a little apprehensive about him getting too comfy after the events that finally transpired on this porch last night. Did he see? Did he hear? Does he know? Was his window open? What's he gonna say? My heart is pumping hard while I just stare at him like a total creeper... anxiously waiting...

"You wanna smoke this with me?" He asks.

Phew, a question I can deal with!

"This early? No thanks. I still have those weed cookies you gave me!"

"NO YOU DON'T!"

Oh hell yes I *do*. Ariah warned me not to eat a whole cookie. I know she said it because I heard her with my *own* ears and fully understood what she said. She didn't lapse into Dothraki – swear it was English. However, in my *mind,* she was talking about a normal, palm-of-your-hand-sized cookie – don't eat the whole thing. Cool, I won't. So when I opened the bag, these tiny cookies were about ¼ of the size of a normal cookie. So in *my* mind, I could eat that whole cookie. So I did; it was a Snickerdoodle and it was crazy tasty. I could've eaten four or five more but thank heavens I stopped at one because apparently, that little ass cookie WAS the whole cookie that I wasn't supposed to eat! That tramp never specified the size of the cookies that she was referencing. I don't remember much after that. There was a lot of laughter and I somehow ended up in my bathtub fully dressed. Not sure why. Not sure how. But I can say that those cookies are still in that cabinet and have remained relatively untouched ever since.

Gabriel's from California with a medical marijuana prescription, so imagine his surprise when he moved to our backward area that has only recently begun to open dispensaries. He lights his joint, which is fine with me because I rather enjoy the smell of it. I'm just not interested in a man who HAS to smoke weed daily to get through his day – not because he needs to but because he just wants to. I once had a man tell me, "It's only weed. If I get pulled over, I just go to jail for a few hours." WTF? As opposed to having *nothing* and getting pulled over and just getting the ticket? Ok...

He hits the joint, "So I gotta question for you. Did you hear a lady screaming last night?"

Shit. I thought I was out of the woods. How the hell am I supposed to respond to THIS!?

"Naahhh..." I reply in a manner that sounds like a total lie. "Screaming, like *screaming*?"

"Yeahhh, I mean it was windy but I coulda swore I heard a woman screaming outside my house. I was concerned! I came down to look but didn't see nothin' though."

"Hmmm... I didn't hear anything, but you know my house is damn near soundproof with this brick and these newer windows. I don't hear much going on outside. Then I usually have the A/C on. Are you sure you weren't just really high?"

"I mean that's a real possibility," he laughs. "I did smoke last night and watched a horror movie."

"See! So you were probably having those auditory hallucinations! Or you were just dreaming."

"Oh, I was awake!" He takes another hit of his item and decides he's done for the moment. "Well either way, if there really *was* a woman, I hope she's ok."

"Well, we haven't seen anything on the news or social media, so it must be all good."

Ugh, this is so embarrassing and an all-time low for me. I am sitting here making an elderly man think he's going crazy when we know damn well he heard a woman ferociously screaming last night. It's just in such poor taste to tell him what his fellow Rican brother was over here doing. One day I'll fess up, but not today.

And that damn Diego, no more outdoor oral events for him. I don't care HOW excited he was by it, he's cut off.

Add to my TO-DO list: Purchase blinds for the porch windows - just in case

CHAPTER 15
Lack of liquor control

DING DING
DING DING

I force my eyes to open so I can look at the clock before finding out who I should be cussin' out for texting me at booty call hours. I ain't givin' up *no* booty so my phone should *not* be dinging this many times. Oh, it's just Mama texting. *Wait, why is she sending me photos?*

DING DING

Ma: Hey Sweets, can you Photoshop these, please? Nip and tuck a few places and do that thing you do to my face. Thanks. Love you.

Out of sheer curiosity, I open one of the photos and instantly feel like I *must* be smack dab in the middle of a hellish nightmare! My mother, who is officially classified as a senior citizen, is incredibly scantily clad and posed like some geriatric Playboy centerfold with a bad hip. Not one, but *four* of these photos are in my phone and will surely cause me to need a great deal of therapy. While this woman neither looks nor acts anywhere near her actual age, I still feel like this must be illegal... or something. My mother is literally sexting me – like, there *has* to be some sort of child abuse law for this.

Renée: Mother! This is disturbing. You can't just send your child sex photos!

Ma: Why? I'm all covered and my CHILD is grown.

Renée: Super not the point!

Ma: Well do u WANT me to have sex or DON'T you?

Renée: OMG! I just don't want you to send it to or discuss it with ME!

Ma: Well I'm SUPPOSED to.

Renée: EW! Yeah, pretty sure that's not how it WORKS! Lol...

With the phone now set to silent, I can no longer be awakened if my mother decides to send any more naughty photos. In the morning, I will edit them but they will only be sent back to her pending a verbal agreement that this is a one-time deal. All future, half-nude images shall be immediately deleted upon receipt and the sender will be blocked – I don't care *how* long she claims her labor was!

♀ ♂ ♀ ♂

Dani and her husband Cade have an adorable home near our office with an amazing pool and deck area. She's been inviting me to come over for a while, but on this 94-degree day, it's time to take her up on that offer. I get the abbreviated tour of the house because Dani is ready to get into the water, but all of it is gorgeous and her backyard is about to be my secret, sacred haven. She doesn't know it yet, but I hope she's not shocked when she comes out here and finds a Black girl floating on one of those inflatable orcas in the pool one morning. The crystal-blue heated water, chaise lounges with umbrellas, fire table, sound system bumping an eclectic variation of music, and the koi pond are all surrounded by giant rocks, trees, and stunning landscaping. She might as well just fix up a room for me.

Cade comes out to introduce himself and when I turn to meet him, well *damn*. A tall, well-sculpted, 50-something, very fetching, silver fox extends his hand for a shake. Well, no wonder Dani is always late for work. I would be late too waking up to this fine specimen of man every day! Everybody in the *house* would be late for something! She may one day grow tired of looking at him, but I'M not yet – I can say that because he's only old enough to be my father if he had me at say, thirteen. So it's all good, right? *Probably not*.

"My goodness, what IS that?" I ask, watching Dani slather herself with a lotion that resembles the consistency of Crisco. "Like 300 SPF? Do you ever *want* to see the sun?"

"Well, I don't wanna burn. What are *you* putting on?"

"Like negative 108 SPF tanning oil. I like to get all sexual chocolate!"

"You can tan?!" she exclaimed, in genuine shock.

"Yes Dani, Black people can tan, and guess what? I just need twelve minutes standing in your pool and I will be an entire shade richer. You won't recognize me if you give me the whole day!"

"I'm not buying that! It takes me *weeks* to tan right and I have to be laid out on TOP of the water at exactly between 11:35 a.m. and 2:12 p.m. with no chance of clouds in the sky! And you're telling me you're gonna do it in twelve minutes standing IN the water?" she scoffs, shaking her head. I smile knowing I will greatly savor the look of incredulous jealousy on her face after she witnesses my glorious quick tan. It's practically a superpower.

Cade is smoking a cigar when he finally hops into the pool with us, and I am loving the smell. Dani tells me that her husband is a cigar connoisseur and has a sizable, well-stocked humidor in the basement. Feeling kind enough to share, Dani rightfully scorns him as he tracks water through the house to grab us both cigars.

"I spend a lot of time at that cigar bar, Maduro," Cade says. "It's *real* nice out there. You ever been?"

"I have actually, but I don't think I enjoyed it as much as you did – I would go back though. Just with different company."

Like a fast-talking, sugared-up six-year-old, the immediate rapid-fire interrogation bombards me. "Oh my gosh! Was it a date? How was it? Was it bad? Did he wear sweatpants? Exactly how many teeth were gold and/or missing?" Dani demanded excitedly. "Babe, she has the *best* worst date stories. Ok, go 'head... *wait*!" She throws up her hands and hurriedly turns back toward the deck. "Lemme get a noodle first."

I am standing in this woman's pool with my mouth ajar, baffled that she would already assume that it was a bad date and irked to have to confirm that she would be correct in that assumption. Not to mention that she and her husband are now both situating their pool floatation devices to get comfortable in preparation for what they are only *presuming* is going to be a juicy story. *Sigh... How is this my life?*

Thomas and I had hung out in the past, but I wasn't feeling much in the way of a romantic connection. Though he was an amazing, well-educated man and had his entire life together, there was just no spark or chemistry. It didn't help that for the first maybe six months of us kind of dating, he never even tried to kiss me. So by the time he had mustered up the gumption to make the attempt, I was feeling only hardcore friend vibes. So it surprised me when, after a year or so of no contact, Thomas reached out and asked if I wanted to go somewhere upscale to smoke cigars. Well, of course I did. I've always enjoyed a good cigar.

I arrived on time at his house, where the plan was for him to drive us the rest of the way in his brand-new Nissan Armada. When car shopping, I considered this SUV and was told that my lease payment would be around $900. So I never even attempted to test drive the damn thing. Finally being able to ride in one had me crazy pumped!

Since stilettos were a part of my attire that evening, Thomas was kind enough to drop me off at the entrance before hunting down a parking space. Maduro, aptly named after one of the most famous dark and flavorsome cigar wrappers, awakened all of the senses upon entering the chic establishment. Targeting a male client base, the barely dressed, but extremely sexy female servers and bartenders stood out among the business casual attire of the male patrons. A live band played in the background while I enjoyed the aroma of random, fragrant cigar flavors as I was escorted to our table.

Thomas arrived shortly after I was seated and promptly ordered a glass of bourbon to accompany the cigars he brought. We lit them up, ordered food, and relaxed in the softly illuminated ambiance of the room while catching up with one another.

By Thomas' third bourbon, I suggested that he maybe not order any additional drinks because not only did he have to drive us home, but he was also starting to say some crazy things to me. I got to hear that his ex-girlfriend was pregnant and due soon but, since she was cheating, he wasn't sure that the baby was his. Since he knew that I wanted children, he said *we* could still have one together – like right now. It would be fine. *No, dude. NOT fine*!

After the fourth bourbon, a $144 bill arrived at our table. I ate $11 sliders and drank water all night, so naturally, I was taken aback when he asked me if I was going to help him out with the bill. *Um. Did I help you drink all that top-shelf bourbon? No? Oh, ok then.* Unable to tell if he was just joking in his drunken state, I informed him that at most, he could get this $20 for my meal and the remainder as gratuity for said meal, and that I would be glad to ask the server to separate the checks. He laughed and declined, which was smart because if he was waiting for ME to cover that bill, he definitely would've been in the back doing dishes to pay off those four $30 glasses of bourbon. Hell, the cost of just that one glass alone could've run my car for a week!

Once the bill had been settled and it was time to go, I learned that standing didn't quite agree with Thomas. All four drinks hit him at once and he instantly became very unsteady, woozy, and unable to explain to me where exactly he parked the car. So we chilled until he felt like he could go find his new truck. As I stood at the curb in front of Maduro with the other patrons awaiting their Ubers and valet parked cars, I saw the large cream SUV approaching, so I stepped forward. Yes, and then I watched him ride RIGHT past me! *OMG! I KNOW this fool is not LEAVING me! Ok, he wouldn't do that, maybe it just wasn't him. But I FEEL like that was him.* Then the truck came back around, passed me in the *other* direction, and stopped. I crossed the street and opened the driver-side door to find him slumped over with his eyes half closed. I told him to give me the keys and get the *fuck* out! And to do it right because the cops were watching.

He looked over and saw two patrol cars facing us, parked like they were just *waiting* for someone to look drunk enough that they could pull over. So Thomas composed himself and faked a sober stroll over to the passenger side while I climbed the eight stairs into this giant boat car. The dashboard on this thing was like an airplane cockpit and this vehicle was easily the size of my basement bathroom! And

I had to drive it back to his house and not wreck it! This is *not* how I envisioned the first driving experience of my dream SUV.

I managed to make it to the highway without incident, which was when I realized I had no actual idea how to get back to his house. As I looked over to get directions, this man was sweating profusely and panting like a hot animal even though it was nowhere near warm outside. So I pressed a variety of buttons which eventually rolled down some windows to get fresh air into the car.

After some twists and turns, I miraculously made it back to his house only to discover the next challenge I'd have to face was parallel parking this behemoth between *my* beautiful sedan and a street light pole. One slip of the wheel and I'd either destroy my baby, take out this retaining wall that I was about to park beside or knock out power to the entire block – all of which would damage this sexy-ass Armada with less than ninety miles on it. He would be pissed, but guess what? He shouldn't have gotten drunk! Fortunately, mama trained me well, and regardless of size, I discovered that I could back that thang up anywhere. Was it as tight as *his* park job would've been? Not at all, but I got a very intoxicated man home safely in the middle of the night driving a giant boat car without wreckage, so it worked for me.

Helping him out of the car proved to be an eventful task considering our size difference. I had to lean this 6' 2", 270lb man against that retaining wall when he began to heave like he was going to be sick. My open-toe shoes were *too* cute that night and had he gotten vomit between my well-pedicured toes, I would've had no other alternative but to mow him down with his *own* boat car! Once the heaving stopped, I helped him up what felt like seventy-eight steps but was probably only about sixteen.

Before allowing him to unlock his door, I felt like we needed to discuss whether or not he knew the code in his drunken state, so he would be able to disarm his alarm system in time. That's *all* I need is for the cops to arrive to find two Black folks in the white part of town with the alarm going off. Like, real talk, we're not tight enough for me to be *that* ride-or-die just yet. He stumbled through the living room, dining room, and finally into the kitchen where the alarm was slowly beeping as I was standing at the entrance waiting. The beeping then accelerated, which put me even more on edge because what was taking so long!? It's four little numbers! Punch them in so we don't get arrested here! It was down to the last maybe ten seconds of the extra quick warning beeps that generally indicate that if you're robbing the place, it's time to leave. Then, as quickly as someone cut the red wire on the bomb, it immediately stopped and I was able to breathe a huge sigh of relief.

He stumbled back into the living room and fell face down onto his leather couch. When asked if this was where he planned to sleep tonight, Thomas replied with a muffled "yes," at which point, I turned out his lights, locked his door, and took my Black ass home! *Why does this crazy always have to happen to me?*

Dani and Cade stare at me with open mouths, the typical response to my escapades.

"So what happened after that?" Cade asked, anxious for the sequel.

"Not a daaamn thing! He called numerous times and later, when I was less pissed, I returned the call. He apologized profusely and we've been just friends ever since. He later admitted that he did wake up and immediately lost all $120 worth of his Bourbon all over his hardwood floor, though."

"Eww, thank God it wasn't carpeted. So was it his baby?" Dani questions.

"Sure was... is... whatever. Li'l Thomas III. Cute li'l thing."

Cade just shakes his head while staring in fascination like I just solved the mystery of the multiverse. "Tell us another one."

I quickly tell them about Phil, who I invited to The Improv to see Eddie Griffin with me. It came to

$85 for the tickets after taxes and fees, but like I said earlier, I have no problem taking a man out. He suggested meeting at Dave & Buster's beforehand, so I agreed. Arriving first and always with a power card in hand, I loaded it up with $25, which I hadn't planned to do. I assumed that since this part was *his* idea, he would cover the games.

Of course, he arrived late, but we played that cash out quickly and had a great time doing so. When I handed him the card to re-load, he suggested leaving and just going to wait for the show to start. I brought up that we wouldn't even need to be in line for about another hour, so I again offered him the card. Reluctantly, he took it and extra slowly re-loaded it – with ten damn dollars. *Um, excuse me sir, WTF are we supposed to do with this for another hour?* He didn't seem interested in loading it again once we finished and I damn sure wasn't about to invest any more of my money, so we left to line up for the show.

I ordered cheese fries and a bottomless lemonade and he ordered something similar while we enjoyed a hilarious show. Toward the end of Eddie's comedic stylings, the server placed the check beside Phil. She came past three times to get it and each time he said, "We're not ready." I was wondering why he wasn't preparing this bill that was only $33, but the show was still going on, so I didn't give it *that* much thought until he leaned in and asked, "Sooo, what are we gonna do about this bill?"

"Um 'scuse me? Who is this '*we*' you speak of? What are YOU gonna do about this bill!? I *paid* for the tickets, I *paid* the bulk of the D&B visit which was YOUR idea, by the way, I *drove* all the way out here and you can't cover my French fries!?"

He told me that he didn't have much money right now because his five kids were about to start school, two of them had football sign-ups, and he was going to Georgia on Monday. My question is, if *that's* the case, why would you accept going out on any date and then suggest additional expensive activities prior, knowing your funds were suspect? I don't go out without either money or some available credit, and if for any reason I *had* to, I would let that person know my situation, just in case.

Again, mouths open. "So, *did* you pay for it?" Cade presses.

"HELL NO she didn't pay for it!" Dani quickly interjects, then looks to me with her eyebrows raised to see if she knows me well enough to have answered that question on my behalf.

"What she just said," I nod in agreement. "I had already spent over $100 on a man who I wasn't even legitimately dating. That was our first and last date."

"So then what happened with the bill if he was so broke?" Cade inquired.

"I honestly have no clue. He went to the back and spoke with someone, presumably trying to work something out or pay with multiple cards? I have no clue – I continued to enjoy the show after I made it clear that at most, I would give him the $10 in cash I had, but no other charges were being made on this credit card tonight. Not cuz I didn't *have* it, but because damn y'all! Anytime a man has *ever* treated me to a comedy show, I *always* covered the food. It's a matter of principle."

"Exactly! He should've told you that he couldn't do it because his funds were going toward the kids that week and allowed you to offer to cover the entire night. Not blindside you at the end of it," Dani added.

"Wow, you just have *all* the luck! Ok one more, tell us another one," Cade requests as they stare at me hopefully with longing eyes.

"Look if I tell you another one, I will feel compelled to send you a bill for this evening's entertainment."

They both laugh but I'm dead ass serious. By the time those stories end, about fifteen minutes have passed, so as promised, I show off my new tan lines to Dani.

"OMG, I HATE you!! That is so not fair!"

Add to my TO-DO list: Stop checkin' out Dani's hot husband and buy an inflatable pool whale

♀ ♂ ♀ ♂

I'm not sure what it is about hanging out in water and sun, but it just zaps all energy and functionality from you. It's only 9:00 p.m. but it's about to be me, the shower, and this bed! And of course, Ariah *would* wait until I'm booty butt naked, ready to hop into this steaming hot water to hit me up. I'm just gonna have to put her on speakerphone while I wash, damn it. Before I can even say hello…

"Oh. My. Gaahhh. BIIITCH!" she whispers, sounding drained of energy.

Aww snap! I know what *this* call is about! Someone finally licked her fudgesicle the *right* way! I told her she would call me when it inevitably happened because she would gain much clearer insight as to my poor decision-making regarding Diego's sexy ass. And I am *so* tickled to finally get this call!

"Bitch! I couldn't git right! No man's ever been able to DO that! I think I even started to stutter," she whispered. "It wasn't natural!"

"Well YAY!!! It's about time! I'm so *happy* for you," I squeal and then lower my tone, "But why are you whispering?"

"He's still here. I just had to run to the bathroom and call you right quick cuz BIIITCH! It was just so good I had to *tell* somebody," she expresses, still whispering.

It must've been spectacular the way she added that bass in her voice when she said "BIIITCH!"

"Ok well get back to it then – it's still early. Have fun!"

I exhale a long, vocal sigh while I think about not only how ecstatic I am for her, but also how I loved being right about it.

Add to my TO-DO list: See if Hallmark makes a "congrats on your new orgasm" greeting card

CHAPTER 16
i don't need your judgy tones

Today is International Renée Day! That's right, my birthday. One year older – no man, no kids, just a bunch of bills. This shit is depressing! Every year my mother calls and sings me Happy Birthday in the morning, but this year I'm waking up to... a text?

Ma: Morning! There's a squirrel outside my kitchen on the roof next door eating a piece of fried chicken. I think it's BBQ.

Shit. I need to call somebody. I think she's going senile! Then the phone rings and her mellifluous voice can be heard singing the song of my birth anniversary. Inevitably, flowers or an edible arrangement will arrive at my home because apparently, my mother is the only person who knows how to romance me since I can't find a man to do the job.

When the doorbell rings, I naturally assume it's the gift from Mama, but to my surprise, Alexis has shown up with gifts, even though she's scheduled to attend my birthday dinner this weekend. What a sweetie!

"I know you like to decorate early for Halloween so I didn't want to wait to get this to you."

True story. My house looks like the whole neighborhood came to visit and everyone got murdered before they could escape. Blood and gore everywhere, to the point that it disturbs the cat and even sometimes scares ME in the middle of the night. I told Mama that this year I wanted to put a corpse on the dining room table. She told me that I could NOT put dead people on my great great great aunt Bertha's antique table. *Um. Hold my beer.* I promptly went to the Halloween store and purchased a life-size skeleton and some human remains for him to eat. So now Earl is positioned on the 96-year-old table in a manner that makes him look like he's trying to rise from the dead. There are spider webs all over him and a human eyeball dangling from his mouth. Needless to say, the cat wants no parts of this dining room.

"You really did it? I thought you were joking about human remains in the house."

"You *know* I don't joke about Halloween OR human remains. He looks good though, huh? His name is Earl."

"You *named* him!? You need help."

"No, I *need* a functional man – cuz this one is starting to look damn good to me. He's great company and listens, ya know? He never interrupts me. And look at those teeth! So straight and white and he always greets me with a smile. And hey, he'll *always* have a boner for me." Wink, wink.

"OMG! Open this gift, weirdo!"

Lexi's Halloween gift bag contains a creepy, aged rotary phone that has a ghoulish voice and says disturbingly haunting things when it's answered. There are also spiders in specimen bottles and a mirror that starts to bleed when someone gets too close. Hot damn! My girl!

"These are awesome! Thank you *so* much! They're goin' up today."

The doorbell rings again and it's a cute, green-eyed FedEx delivery man smiling sweetly at my very married friend. *This* must be my gift from my mother. Lexi signs for it, completely oblivious to the fact that she was being eyed up.

"Is this the package you were expecting from your mom? Open it, I'm nosey."

You never have to tell *me* twice to open a gift, but maybe Lexi should've in this case. This large brown box contains that under-the-bed, four-point restraint system that I was checking out with Ariah a few months back. There is also a whip, blindfold, nipple clamps with purple bells, a cock ring, and a tube of anal ease. Lexi and I both silently stand in the kitchen, heads tilted, with bewildered looks on our faces. I don't think either of us was expecting this. Lexi picks up the small package containing the black rubber ring.

"What do you *do* with this?" she frowns.

"I have *no* clue. I don't think this is from my mother?"

"That *can't* be from your mom," she immediately follows. "Diego maybe?"

We begin to rifle through the box to find a card, but nothing. Who would send a gift like this with *no* card? When the phone rings and it's my sister's face on the screen, I realize that if not Diego, this has Neka written all over it.

"AAAAAAAYYYYY SISS!!" she shouts with her tongue out. "Happy Birthday! I got an email that my package was delivered! You open it?"

"It's... interesting. I'm just glad it wasn't from my mother. We would've had to have a serious talk! But thank you? I think?"

"You're welcome. Lemme know when Diego comes to wear that ass *out*! Oh crap, gotta call you back! This damn kid is drawing on the wall with markers! You want a child so bad? TAKE THIS ONE!"

Lexi and I giggle as we hear her chasing down my niece before she officially hangs up the video call.

"I should've asked *her* freaky ass what to do with this ring thing."

"RIGHT!? C'mon, let's go put this on the bed – it looks fun," she says, heading to my stairs.

"NOW!?"

"Absolutely, you're gonna need help."

Lex and I stand at the foot of my beautifully made queen size bed, elevated on risers for your royal highness. We're trying to figure out how to put these large black sex restraints on a classy, elegant, gold bed covered in shams, large square cushions, and decorative pillows, without wrecking or unmaking the bed. I'm mildly disturbed by how quickly she comes up with a very sensible plan to use the arm restraints to slide it up between the mattress and box spring. I suspiciously feel like she may have *done* this before. We adjust the length of the restraints and tuck them under the mattress so I won't look like a super chic freak when people visit.

"There. Now you just need a man," she says with a satisfied smile on her face. If only it were that easy.

What a weekend full of birthday fun! Seventeen friends accompanied me to the ever so classy Atiya's Grille to celebrate – I turned thirty again, and I've decided to continue to turn thirty until I look forty-eight, or until Karen the cake lady looks at me funny.

Unfortunately, the fine dining establishment was hosting a reception that ran late, so they supplied us with multiple glasses of wine to appease us while we waited. Because we were there for dinner, that meant we were all drinking on empty stomachs. So by the time they seated us, we were ALL three sheets to the wind, except for Lexi – she rarely drinks so she's my designated driver for the evening.

I ordered an octopus tentacle dish as an appetizer. So yeah, I was pretty blitzed. According to Blaire, whenever the server placed it down in front of me, the horrified look on my face was priceless as I first examined it thoroughly, then carefully jabbed at it with a fork for a few minutes, asking loudly why it was "so tight." Keeping my distance, in case it made a grab for my fork, I tentatively took the world's smallest bite. With my best martyred face, and eyebrows furrowed in deep concentration, I valiantly yet painfully chewed a few times on the rubbery texture before declaring it was safe to eat! I don't recall all of the events due to my alcohol-induced haze, but she says I proceeded to then bitch and moan that everybody else tasted it only after I, as the Guinea pig, had deemed it safe and palatable. I would definitely order it again, believe it or not.

Lexi later told me that after hitting my sister's blunt in the parking lot, I talked the entire half-hour ride home about nonsense. I wasn't sure that I believed her when she said I removed my shoes and walked barefoot to my house because I don't even walk around *inside* my home without socks or slippers. But when I woke up wearing very little and found a trail of my clothes leading from my bedroom downstairs to the front door, it all sounded pretty plausible. Fortunately, I'm not feeling any residual effects of the drinking, which is good because I have a date-type/outing-type situation thing today. In my confusion, I don't even know what to call them anymore because they are serving me no purpose.

This crisp, fall Sunday afternoon is perfect for fro-yo in the park. There's a nice breeze, which is helpful should Aron's breath be as tragic as my *last* fro-yo date's. I take a seat on the park bench and await his arrival, hoping that he picked up on the fact that we would be meeting in a higher-end part of town and would dress accordingly. But alas, why would I bother hoping for such a thing? As I cross the street to meet him, I take note of his jeans with the four neon yellow reflective stripes paired with a yellow and blue plaid button-down, covered by a red, black, and white leather jacket. This unique ensemble is topped off with a black skull cap, blue shades, and shoes that don't match a damn thing. They're not even in the same genre of clothing he's wearing, whatever *that* is.

Once we order, he suggests taking a walk through the quaint town. I agree, even though I feel like he needs to remove half the clothing he's wearing. Aron talks *so* much that it is pointless to try to get a word in edgewise, so I just walk with him and listen to all the misogynistic trash fall out of his mouth and have my own conversation in my mind. The familiar tug-of-war between my shoulder angel and shoulder devil make their inevitable mental appearance as I count to ten and walk this razor's edge of control. But I can almost assure you that since I haven't mastered the whole poker face yet, the expressions are likely priceless. This will be a quick walk because I'm losing patience already.

"You're *very* nice looking. Honestly, I'm surprised you're as pretty as you are because the farther you get from the coast, normally the fatter and uglier the women get."

"Thank you?"

Wow. I find this amusing because YOU are no visual prize your damn self. I'm 5'8" and you're... definitely not. Your thighs appear to rub together more than most of the thick chicks I know and those poor buttons on that shirt around your midsection are holding on for dear life! Your facial hair doesn't even grow in evenly. So how are YOU talking about fat and ugly women when your beard doesn't even connect!? My shoulder devil purrs and cracks her knuckles in preparation for the coming catastrophe bound to arise. The angel tries to calm me down and reminds me it's almost over.

Since we're walking in the direction of my car, I decide to toss my wristlet and shades into the center console while Aron stands nearby, squinting skeptically at my beautiful clean baby.

"Oh…" he remarks with heavy judgment. "*That's* your car huh? It's… cute."

Cute? You MUST be on drugs. Baby Girl here is fully loaded aggressive sex on wheels. We don't DO cute here. I could ask what you drive but after you've just insulted her, I really don't care. Shoulder angel applauds my taking the high road while the devil considers smacking the shades off of his stupid face.

So we keep walking, he keeps talking and I keep staring at him like he's crazy.

"I'm not accustomed to dating regular women. I'm used to dating doctors and lawyers, but here, I only get approached by teachers and nurses."

Umm, so that's pretty offensive, considering I also teach college part-time. I, of course, wouldn't expect you to know that since you haven't asked me anything about myself because you just keep TALKING! But either way, nurses and teachers are both highly educated and we don't need YOU to pay our bills, so what is wrong with dating one of us? Also, what doctor would WANT you other than to put you on some form of medication? And there are probably a dozen attorneys RIGHT now objecting to your trash-ass statements, sir.

"I dropped the extra "A" from Aaron because I wanted to make a statement. Be different – a unique specimen."

Oh, you're some sort of specimen all right. One that might need to be studied somewhere so they could figure out if science has advanced enough to shut you the hell up for five minutes.

"Yeah I don't cook. I don't need to because whatever woman I marry will handle all of that."

Oh word? She's gonna handle ALL of it, huh? The doctor or lawyer you marry will work a 14-hour shift then come home and cook your meal? Lemme know how that works out for you. It's beyond time to end this walk.

On the way back to the fro-yo shop, we approach Aron's car, which he is SO proud to display. He says, "I drive a Jag" with an arrogant, "My car is better than yours" tone.

I'm looking for it but all I see are a shiny black Volvo, a hunter BMW and a pearl Audi. Beside them, destroying the optics is a silver sedan with a donut on the rear passenger side and a handicap sticker dangling off the rearview mirror.

"Yeeah, that's my sexy right *there*," he says, rubbing his hands together and beaming with pride. I'm still looking around the parking lot for the Jag.

Wait you're trying to call THAT a Jaguar? And you put a handicap sticker in the front, really!? That would totally be wrecking the elegance of the car if there WERE any. And WHY? You're not handicapped? Wait, never mind. You CLEARLY need that sticker because something is definitely wrong with you in the head.

As we get closer, it's evident that this is not even a *new* Jag - it's like the first Jag ever made! I look inside and the tan leather is dry and cracked and it has a *tape deck*! Stop it! And where is the cat? There is supposed to be a sophisticated feline hood ornament gracefully leaping off the front of this vehicle, the primary recognition symbol of a Jaguar. Oh, no cat? No jag emblem? It broke off? Oh, ok Aron. You know they'll send you a new one if you just give them your credit card number, right? Normally I'm not too judgmental when it comes to what type of car a man is driving, but given that he had the audacity to look upon *my* new car with judgment, I'm judging *back*, damn it!! How about go find the extra "A" in your name *and* the car's emblem and drive that rusted-out shit box back to the coast to find that doctor to cook your dinner. Thank you and good night.

All this goes through my mind while standing in front of this alleged Jaguar because I would never actually *say* it. That's not nice. Not sure why Aron thought it would make sense to attempt to go in for a kiss, but I Harlem Globetrotted my way right out of that and instead, he got the church hug - that one where only the upper bodies touch.

"All those people are looking at you," he says, unable to resist declaring one last narcissistic jab.

And there's my limit. My shoulder angel is pulling her hair back and taking off her earrings, threatening, "If you don't tell THIS west coast, simple motherfucker where to go..."

"Yeah, see no. They're looking at *you*."

I'm dressed appropriately and YOU, sir, look like you're about to steal little fluffy over there and you know white people don't play about their dogs!

Add to my TO-DO list: Find a therapist because maybe I'M the one going crazy here

CHAPTER 17
questioning my sanity

Holy shit. I'm now on my third counselor – this is starting to look like my dating life. I didn't realize that finding a good therapist would be as difficult as finding a good man. I can see how talking to someone and working out any issues would be beneficial. However, I prefer to find someone who looks like me and can relate to my particular brand of struggle in terms of dating, fertility, job stress, etc... I just want one Black, female mental health professional who can figure out if I am the reason that these crazy ass men seem to magnetically gravitate to me. Apparently, I must've asked for a purple unicorn with pink leopard spots.

There is such a stigma surrounding Black people seeking therapy, but it does help when you find the right person. If we can see doctors for our physical health and well-being, why should becoming mentally healthy be looked upon any differently? But again, without the right person, you can leave just as messed up as you came in, which I did.

My first counselor seemed cool but then she started telling me about HER problems! Hello? She's supposed to be the professional here! I shouldn't know about her husband's problems, her sister's kids, the nephews she had to adopt, the shitty tenants in her rental property, etc... I should've been sending *her* a bill! But then one day I was venting, thinking I was talking to her confidentially as a professional and she went and told the person I was venting about everything I said. I feel like surely that's a HIPAA violation and I should've filed a complaint, but I didn't.

I took a break until I could find someone more functional, but that never happened. The next one was an older Black woman who was very kind, but she liked to discuss current events, Black history, HBCU education, *her* history, *her* family - ya know, all things that I wasn't there to discuss. Then when we *did* discuss things I needed to talk about, she would Google them and read them to me. WTF? I was once in a very dark place and what I *didn't* need was this nice lady reading to me "The Top Ten Reasons Why You Shouldn't Commit Suicide." Because the reality was, sitting through that was the #1 reason I *wanted* to commit suicide that day. I called her when I lost my entire mind and stood in my dining room with scissors and cut off *all* but three inches of my beautiful hair. I left that session feeling no better than I did when I entered it. So as sweet as she was, her methods were not effective either.

Third time's a charm? Though I honestly don't know how much it's helping, this counselor is far more functional than the previous two and only mentions personal things when they are relevant to the subject at hand. Even then, they're brief, which is appreciated because this isn't *about* her right now. She seems pleased with my overall awareness of how the relationship with my father is affecting my tolerance level with men, but it becomes increasingly clear that the stress of my workplace is my primary need for our visits. The tension and anxiety are having a trickle-down effect on my overall mood, which in turn affects how I process and react to information, which in essence affects *all* of my interactions.

Today she and I are discussing Santos, his ex, and his baby mama who have more drama than ABC on a Thursday night. I don't even know what Santos looks like in person because we've never gotten to meet. Though he informed me that he would be the end to my life's tragic dating story, it's not looking promising. We exchanged messages online, talked on the phone and video chatted, but in just ONE week since my last session, an entire season of some sort of urban drama unfolded to the point where I was ready to cancel my *actual* cable! My therapist just stares at me stupefied and doesn't have much in the way of helpful insight.

Day one

Santos and I had a two-hour-long conversation that went really well and his deep, thick voice with the sexy Puerto Rican accent was nice to listen to. He asked if I had ever dated a Puerto Rican before – uhhh, not *dated,* exactly. He didn't need to hear about *that* part of my life right then. He expressed to me how beautiful I was, how he was so shocked that I could still be single, and how hard it was to find intelligent, functional women here who have their lives together. He told me about his daughter who looks just like him, the relationship between him and her mother, and we discussed our previous relationships. His most recent ex didn't work or go to school. She just hung out and he pretty much took care of all the financials for her and her three children. I'm sure that gets old fairly quickly, and as for the baby mama, she has a career but is dating a bum-ass dude, smokes a ton of weed, and isn't that fiscally responsible.

From what I'm told, there is a vast difference between what a man considers "his baby mama" and "his child's mother." His child's mother has her life together and can effectively communicate, take care of their child, makes her own money, and is responsible with those funds in addition to the child support coming into the home. The baby mama on the other hand? She's usually the total opposite of that previous description and is usually full of all of the drama and makes one literally question this man's taste in women. In the past, I haven't minded dealing with men with children who have a purposeful co-parent. But when it comes to having all the baby mama drama, fighting, constant court visits, spiteful behavior, etc...? I just can't do it. Santos confirmed that would not be the case.

Day two

Baby Mama's washer was broken so instead of her bum ass dude getting it fixed or her using the damn near $1,000 a month she's getting in child support to buy another one, she has been doing all her and their daughter's laundry at Santos' house. Oh, and asking to borrow the car which he figured maybe he should just *give* to her. *Interesting.*

Around 11 p.m. Santos' other phone began to ring... and ring... and ring constantly. He got off the phone with me to take this call from her because he said she would just keep calling until he answered. Nothing was wrong with the teenage daughter, this was just standard behavior because *no* limitations have been set with this woman. So from *my* perspective, it looks as though she feels like she can pretty much do and take whatever.

Day three

I was chatting with Santos and he informed me that his baby mama was asleep on his couch. What the actual fuck? Am I crazy? She was borrowing the car later today also. Not sure how her dude was okay with her constantly over another man's house, especially her ex, and driving his car? But okay.

Nighttime fell, and we were engaged in another deep conversation. Once again, the phone began to ring... and ring... and ring... He again, got off the phone with *me* to take this call from *her*, which I felt was so disrespectful, given the late hour. *No* woman wants to feel like the man she's trying to date is prioritizing another woman for no particular reason. If there were ongoing issues with their child, that would be one thing. But because she's spoiled and seems to want his attention when she wants it? No. How about let's go get a Webster's Dictionary and look up the word "boundaries" please.

Day four

I got a phone call from Santos telling me about how his baby mama smoked weed in his car when she took it. Wow. I always thought you were supposed to treat other people's belongings better than you would treat your own. So the fact that she would smoke weed in somebody's car who doesn't smoke weed themselves is pretty discourteous. But she had a death in the family so we're giving her a pass, I guess.

She wanted to stay with him and sleep on the couch that night. He said he didn't want her to and asked me what he should do. I reminded him that he's a grown-ass man so he's going to do whatever he wants but, be prepared that if she's feeling vulnerable, she's not going to want to be alone and she would likely end up in his bed. Yes, even though she has her own bum-ass dude. Why the hell will this chick not go *home*? He said he told her that she couldn't stay, but I don't know if that was really how it went down - or if she really even left.

Day five

I got a phone call early in the morning, but it only rang once so I was wondering who could it be. The caller ID didn't pick it up, but fortunately, I have an app for that. I opened it and I saw an area code that was the same as Santos', yet it wasn't his number. There was a woman's name associated with these digits. So I, being the savvy investigative reporter that I am, opened up his social media page and looked through his friends list. Sure enough, I found the same woman's name – his ex who is still across the state. I called him and of course, he didn't answer. Angry about that call, I messaged him and asked why his bitches are calling my house. I figured that would get his attention. When he called back, seemingly confused, he claimed to have no idea how it happened and that he wasn't sure how she even got my number. Eventually, he apologized, but it took way longer than it should've.

Day six

Santos called numerous times to apologize for the fact that he has no boundaries set between him and his baby mama *or* his ex who called my house. I haven't even *met* this man yet and already there is way too much drama for me in addition to there being too many women involved in our thing we're potentially trying to create. He once asked if I was a jealous person and my answer to that was, no not generally, but I am a *tired* person. I am tired of this craziness and foolery with men. I literally bring *no* drama or baggage to my relationships, yet I am somehow constantly having to battle everyone else's. I'm too old for this.

Day seven

Ya know, when we should be resting... Santos was still calling to apologize. Finally, by nightfall, he decided to leave yet another voicemail with another apology. Upon listening to this message, I felt bad and decided to actually return his call. I cannot make this up - when I dialed his number back, a *woman* answered. I just hung up, because I'm not here for verbal sparring with a woman who shouldn't even be on my phone.

Why did he spend a day and a half trying to apologize to me only to have another chick answer the phone? Why does this woman, whom he says he doesn't want, feel like she is entitled enough to be able to answer HIS phone? I officially called it quits before I even ever got to meet the man - lose my number, please. He claimed that he wasn't with his baby mama that night and that his ex somehow answered the call from across the state by hacking into his phone. Regardless of which story anyone believes, none of this was okay. You can't start a relationship with that much drama and expect it to magically disappear once you've decided you're an item.

"I… am not really sure how to respond to any of that. I mean that's a LOT," the counselor says while giggling and shaking her head. Another common response.

Rarely is she at a loss for words, though I sense she's glad that she doesn't have to spend time counseling me to see that I deserve better than putting up with that BS. But regardless, I will continue my journaling and see what comes of it.

♀ ♂ ♀ ♂

Following my therapist's advice to do some reflecting, I sit on my porch watching the changing leaves blow in the wind. I realize it's been just over one year since touring this house and deciding to make it my home. I think about how much of a blessing it was to be able to get a loan so quickly and not have to work on my credit, which enabled me to rapidly get out of my trashy living situation. Spending the past year actually liking my neighbors in peace and quiet has been rejuvenating to my spirit and soul. While I haven't found my soulmate to christen all of the rooms in this big ass house or the floor by the fireplace, I at least got this porch partially knocked off the bucket list.

A smile crosses my face as I think about all the fun memories that were created during my first year of home ownership. I should probably follow through with getting those locks changed before a hoard of people come over and start making *new* memories while I'm not even home. Who knows how many of them mysteriously ended up with keys?

"Why you sittin' there smiling all goofy?" yells a voice from a familiar muscle car.

"Wouldn't you like to know..."

Diego backs up from the stop sign and attempts to park his car again – still so badly. I cringe when I hear the tires and beautiful chrome rims scratch the side of the curb and fully understand when I hear him screaming every variation of the "F" word he can create in various languages. He gets out to assess the damage then takes all his anger out on the overly tight hug he gives me. No man should look that sexy in a simple black Adidas tee, but he is giving me snack-like, eye-candy vibes all day with those huge arms damn near busting out of those tight short sleeves.

Diego takes a seat on the other side of the fire table and lights it. The flames flicker in his hazel eyes as he smiles at me and takes me in like I'm the most perfect thing he's seen all day. *I'm not.* I'm rocking my standard grey sweat suit and ponytail, wearing no make-up. I feel like I could star in The Walking Dead. But since my esthetician, Marcia, did such an excellent job on my brows, those are the only presentable things on me right now.

"Was you thinkin' about me?" he asks.

"No," I shake my head answering honestly.

"Wowww! Break a dude's heart. Ok, well I was thinkin' bout'chu. Ummm... I been wantin' ta talk ta you cuz I got some things to say, but... you know... Ummm...”

I can't help but to smirk because whatever this is, it's kind of adorable. Diego is usually so self-assured and borderline cocky. So to see him all fidgety, flustered, and flushed is incredibly abnormal and cute. I don't want to make him even more uncomfortable than he already seems to be so I try to get this face under control and wait for him to finish articulating his thoughts.

“Ummm... Necesito tu confianza,” he says, choosing to speak Spanish when he's uncomfortable with vocalizing his thoughts in English.

“I need... your... confidence? No... trust? Is that what you said?”

“Si! Look at'chu! Tu Español está mejorando! We gon be havin' whole conversations en Español soon!”

I smile blankly as to not let him know that I have no *clue* what “mejorando” means so I will just google it when he leaves. But it must be good because he sounds exceedingly proud.

“So... I wanna take you out. What do you think?”

“Take me out? As in what? Shoot me?”

“No silly, like a date... Ya know?” he says, still squirmy and rattled as though he's never asked a woman out before.

"In public? What about your flavor of the month?"

"I'm not seein' anybody. It's jus' me right now. For real."

I don't believe that for a minute because I've heard that story too many times. Diego once left my house and I later found out he was *engaged*! It broke my heart because I was really feeling him back then. But ever since that betrothal ended, Diego literally always has a woman at-bat, one on deck, and at least a few others in the dugout. And don't even get me started on what fan girls are in the bleachers. I have no idea how to classify myself in that scenario because we've never been in a relationship, we're not dating or even having actual sex. What I *do* know is that I'm no one's "next to bat" bitch. I'm the MVP and I can't date anyone who doesn't treat me as such because I will always treat my man that way.

"But uhhh, you know, I jus' wanted to say that ummm... I enjoy your company an' stuff. I like being wit'chu an' I *know* I ain't been the most honest in the past. I lied. I came ta see you when I was in relationships that I told you I wasn't in, which I know, makes me a cheater an' ummm... you have *no* reason ta trust me. I *know* this. I don't deserve your trust but I wanna earn it. If you'll let me. I wanna work ta earn your trust an' respect."

Here I go again lookin for Ashton to see if I'm being Punk'd because *really? Maybe Diego has a camera in his lapel. Shit, he's wearing a T-shirt.* I am at such a loss right now because I have *no* idea how I should or want to respond to this request. It sounds nice in theory, but can a man so accustomed to lying and infidelity change that much? I fear that this man, who I legitimately care about, will leave me all sprung out and broken-hearted in need of even more therapy. Hell, I would need it anyway because how could I manage my insecurity regarding this man? I feel so flawed in comparison to his physical perfection and I would always think he's lying to or cheating on me.

As the master of playing it cool, I casually reply, "Ohh wow, that's a lot... but respectable. So how do you plan to do that? The whole earning back trust thing?"

"Sooo, hadn't really thought about the *how*," he laughs, showing off that beautiful grin. "I guess by followin' through on what I say I'm gon' do. Let my actions speak more than my words. *Show* you I care, *show* you I'm doin' right. Try ta just be more... consistent – keep in touch better, ya know. An' just tell you the truth even if it's some shit you don't wanna hear. You'll know I'm bein' honest. Quiero que confíes en mi."

I have to pause to translate before replying since I'm still learning. Plus, his deep voice speaking Spanish is just *really* such a distraction because it's so damn sexy. But I feel comfortable enough with my translation to reply, "I wanna trust you too, Diego."

Usually, the only time this man looks me in the eyes is when he's about to do something horribly pleasurable to my body. Even when we're fully engaged in deep conversation, I only typically receive partial eye contact. So the fact that he's looking at me now with such serious intensity, he appears to be genuine in his request. I've never seen him be this open about his feelings and so vulnerable.

"I'm so confused. Where did all this even *come* from? Are you terminal and need a caretaker or something?" I asked, getting as flustered as he is.

"I was in the gym liftin' and it jus' hit me like damn, I'm always thinkin' about'chu. That smile. The way we *laugh* together. You're jus' so smart and sexy... and..."

"See I can't with you cuz you're lyin' *already*! Knowin' damn well I'm out here, no make-up on looking like the crypt keeper right now."

"*Stop* it. I love that you don't wear all'at make-up, fake lashes, fake hair, an' shit. You're real an' it's sexy. I love when you rock your natural curls an' when you look at me through dark brown eyes. Yeah, the green contacts are sexy as hell, but you don't need 'em."

Really I do, they're prescription. Ugh, he's sayin' all the right things but I just can't allow myself to get hurt again. Diego *will* inevitably hurt me – it's only a matter of when. I feel like I need to call someone and get some feedback on what to do. But I already know that half of the posse will say let him try, the other half will say not to go there and Desirée will start hunting for a whole chicken's foot to enact a curse that causes both of his eyebrows to grow together.

"Well, thank you for the compliment and the sweet, yet kinda unbelievable words, though I'm still not sure how to respond. But I *do* wanna know what's in the bag."

"Oh, this?" He smiles proudly as he removes the items one by one to artfully display them. "Just some chocolate bars... marshmallows... an' graham crackers," he smiles even bigger. "And this."

"Ahhh my purple vitamin water!" I squeal with glee. "That's so cute! Thank you!"

"I don' know how to pronounce this 'aakai' shit, but I was listenin' ta you." *He means açaí.* "It was the only purple one there. And I know you been wantin' ta make some s'mores so..."

That's really cute and *so* sweet that he was paying attention - maybe there's some hope for him yet. Diego and I sit outside at the fire table making s'mores, even though he doesn't usually eat junk food, and talking for hours into the night. Then of course you know what happens next...

Well... that too, but I was also finally made passionate (and kinky) love to; that's just how he rolls, but it definitely lasted longer than two strokes! There were no accidents and nothing weird got licked that wasn't *supposed* to, so I will call this romantic liaison a success. Frankly, it's scary that those are my criteria for success here.

Can I learn to trust Diego? Only time will tell. But in the meantime, I have a call to make because damn, that sex wasn't bad! *Who can I call? Brie this time. But she'll probably be mad too. Nah, sex is involved, she'll be cool.*

"BITCH! It is three in the morning!" Brie groggily snaps.

Oh, damn maybe not.

"Girl, I just had sex so fire we *may* need to evacuate the building and call the bomb squad," I whisper.

"Oh shit! I'm up, I'm up! Scale of 1-10? How many stars?"

"Oh Uhh, 8.5, 4-stars," I answer thoughtfully.

"So did he land the dismount?"

"Brie, what the *hell* kinda freaky do y'all be *doin'* in that bed!?" I ask laughing. "OMG, I don't wanna know, I gotta go," I say still giggling as I hang up.

Add to my TO-DO list: See how Diego feels about this ball gag

THE END

SEE WHAT HAPPENS NEXT IN

Soulmate Setbacks: Confessions II

If you've enjoyed my little slice of crazy, reviews on **Amazon** and **Goodreads** are incredibly helpful to authors. Please and thank you!

Keep an eye out for my upcoming psychological crime thriller, *Stolen Pieces*, scheduled to release in June of 2023.

ACKNOWLEDGMENTS

To my readers, it is so incredibly scary to put your personal life out in these literary streets. So, thank you for spending your time with me and allowing me to tell these wild stories. I appreciate you.

For inspiration, ideas, memories, and support, I would like to thank Crystal, Ellise, Edmund, Kathryn, Clarence, Rafael, Rebecca, Jocelyn, Jennifer, Cindy, and Percida. Thank you.

A special thanks to Kimberly Reszetylo for doing things to this book that others should've done before her.

ABOUT THE AUTHOR

J.R. Mason often wonders how sane she really is... especially after putting all of this wildness in writing.

Mason received her Bachelor of Arts in Journalism & Mass Communication from Cleveland State University and her Master of Arts in Advertising/Graphic Design/Public Relations from Point Park University. A full-time marketing specialist position, along with running a freelance design company keeps her quite busy and leaves little free time for her guilty pleasures – movies and massages!

This Ambridge, PA native also takes joy in playing her trumpet, screenplay writing, travel, outdoor fires on cool nights (obviously), anything with sugar in it, and reading erotica or psychological thrillers.

Contact:
Order signed copies: jrenecreative.com/confessions
Follow me on IG: author_j.r.mason